The Legend of Herostratus

University of Florida Monographs
Humanities No. 45

The Legend of Herostratus

Existential Envy
in Rousseau and Unamuno

Gregory L. Ulmer

A University of Florida Book

The University Presses of Florida
Gainesville · 1977

Library of Congress Cataloging in Publication Data

Ulmer, Gregory L.   1944–
    The legend of Herostratus.

    (University of Florida humanities monograph; no. 45)
    "A University of Florida book."
    Includes bibliographical references.
    1. Unamuno y Jugo, Miguel de, 1864–1936.
2. Rousseau, Jean Jacques, 1712–1778. I. Title.
II. Series: Florida. University, Gainesville.
University of Florida monographs : Humanities ; no. 45.
B4568.U54U43   868'.6'209 [B]   77-22363
ISBN 0-8130-0567-1

Acknowledgments

If print immortalizes, then let me mention here the names of several of those whom I would like remembered for their generosity in helping me in one way or another, and in more ways than one, with this project: Juan López-Morillas, Bob Scholes, Alistair Duckworth, Antonio Sánchez Barbudo, Gregor Sebba, Gareth Schmeling; and, for her support and understanding, my wife, Kathy.

Additional thanks must go to the University of Florida Graduate School for making possible the publication of this monograph.

For LAVONNE and WALTER

Contents

ABBREVIATIONS OF AUTHORS' WORKS (MODERN EDITIONS) CITED IN THE TEXT

Jean-Jacques Rousseau

C   *Les Confessions* (Paris: Garnier, 1964).
CS   *Du Contrat Social* (Paris: Garnier, 1962). Includes *Discours 1, Discours 2, Lettre à M. d'Alembert, Contrat Social, Gouvernement de Pologne, Lettre à Mgr. de Beaumont.*
D   *Rousseau Juge de Jean-Jacques: Dialogues* (Paris: Armand Colin, 1962).
E   *Emile ou de l'Education* (Paris: Garnier, 1964).
M   "Lettres" to Malesherbes, in *Correspondence Générale de J.-J. Rousseau*, ed. Theophile Dufour, 20 vols. (Paris: Armand Colin, 1924–34), vol. 7.
OC   *OEuvres Complètes*, ed. Bernard Gagnebin and Marcel Raymond, 4 vols. to date (Paris: Gallimard, 1959–).
Rev   *Les Rêveries du Promeneur Solitaire* (Paris: Garnier, 1960).

Miguel de Unamuno

AC   *La Agonía del Cristianismo* (Buenos Aires: Losada, 1966).
AP   *Amor y Pedagogía* (Madrid: Espasa-Calpe, 1964).
AS   *Abel Sánchez* (Madrid: Espasa-Calpe, 1965).
CSH   *Como se hace una novela* (Madrid: Alianza, 1966).
DQ   *Vida de Don Quijote y Sancho* (Madrid: Espasa-Calpe, 1966).
EN   *Ensayos*, ed. Bernardo G. de Candamo, 2 vols. (Madrid: M. Aguilar, 1942).
ETC   *En Torno al Casticismo* (Madrid: Espasa-Calpe, 1964).
N   *Niebla* (Madrid: Taurus, 1965).
O   *"El Otro" y "El Hermano Juan"* (Madrid: Espasa-Calpe, 1964).
OCs   *Obras Completas*, ed. Manuel García Blanco, 5 vols. (Madrid: Afrodisio Aguado, 1950–52).
PG   *Paz en la Guerra* (Madrid: Espasa-Calpe, 1964).
SM   *"San Manuel Bueno, Mártir" y Tres Historias Más* (Madrid: Espasa-Calpe, 1963).
ST   *Del Sentimiento Trágico de la Vida* (Buenos Aires: Losada, 1964).
TNE   *Tres Novelas Ejemplares y un Prólogo* (Madrid: Espasa-Calpe, 1965).

Ecce homo

Ja! Ich Weiss, woher ich stamme!
Ungesättigt gleich der Flamme
Glühe und verzehr' ich mich.
Licht wird alles, was ich fasse,
Kohle alles, was ich lasse:
Flamme bin ich sicherlich!

FRIEDRICH NIETZSCHE
Die Fröhliche Wissenschaft

He who pursues fame at
the risk of losing his self is not
a scholar.
CHUANG TZU (369–286 B.C.)

Introduction: Unamuno and the Genevans

> *Every writer creates his own*
> *precursors.*
> JORGE LUIS BORGES

It is difficult to think of Miguel de Unamuno the writer without thinking of him at the same time as a reader, a prodigious reader, master of nine languages, professor of classical philology, university president, philosopher, a reader by profession. Our purpose will be to reconstruct, at least in one specific context, the reading figure present in the pages of Unamuno's writings, pages set deliberately into a network of references, allusions, and citations which are often unacknowledged, distorted, or taken out of context. A phrase is not the possession of the one who "invents" it, he says, but of the one who uses it to the best advantage (OCs, 9: 750). Necessarily so, since "thought, reason, that is, living language, is an inheritance" (ST, p. 271). Thus the reader Unamuno's "stolen speech" dominates the writer's language. His method is hermeneutical in the traditional sense, producing works which tend to be commentaries on other works.

We now suspect that everyone writes this way, webbed in tradition like this professor, that speech speaks us, that we are written. "Everything is for us books, reading," Unamuno declares (CSH, p. 129). "Intertextuality" is the term now used to describe the relations among written works for which the author is a mere conductor, a producer rather than a creator. Although the theory of textuality is a recent development, Unamuno anticipates it, along with other aspects of current reader-oriented theories, in intersubjectivity—a phenomenology of reading—of which he was one of the earliest practitioners. We shall limit ourselves here, however, to a consideration of Unamuno as a critic of conscious-

1

ness, as an intersubjective reader. Applying his own methods of sympathetic reading, we will define specifically how and why Unamuno read Jean-Jacques Rousseau—what, as an active, even aggressive reader, he learned from Rousseau, and how this lesson appears in his own writing.

The question that perhaps ought to be addressed before any other concerns the relationship itself: why, among all the possibilities, should we focus on Unamuno's relationship with Rousseau? Unamuno himself, of course, makes the connection when he describes the tradition to which he belongs. Before defining his famous tragic sense of life—an awareness of "the eternal and tragic contradiction [between our emotions and our reason], the basis of our existence" (ST, p. 20)—Unamuno offers a list of figures both fictional and historical who represent a tradition of this awareness, including "Marcus Aurelius, Saint Augustine, Pascal, Rousseau, *René, Obermann,* Thomson, Leopardi, Vigny, Lenau, Kleist, Amiel, Quental, Kierkegaard" (ST, p. 22).[1] He specifies the kind of men he admires, and again Rousseau is included: "Dante, Luther, Jean-Jacques, are the great rebels of their respective centuries . . ." (EN, 2:1104). These rebels—"religious spirits, men of passion and faith, of enthusiasm"—are contrasted with a type for whom Unamuno has no sympathy, that is, the rationalists, the skeptics, the "Voltaires" of the world.

As youthful Rousseauists, Unamuno and his friends, wearing peasant sandals, would climb the mountains near Bilbao—Archanda and Iturriogorri—to predicate a "romantic anti-urban-

---

1. The "tragic" contradiction is methodological as well as metaphysical and is part of Unamuno's anticlassicism. "Suele buscarse la verdad completa en el *justo medio* por el método de remoción, *via remotionis,* por exclusión de los extremos, que con su juego y acción mutua engendran el ritmo de la vida, y así solo se llega a una sombra de verdad, fría y nebulosa. Es preferible, creo, seguir otro método, el de afirmación alternativa de los contradictorios; es preferible hacer resaltar la fuerza de los extremos en el alma del lector para que el medio tome en ella vida, que es resultante de lucha." *En Torno Al Casticismo* (Madrid, 1964), p. 15. Rousseau's method is exactly the same: "Par un autre biais, le texte de Rousseau est un piège: sa méthode d'analyse reste délibérément antinomique. Il y a dans l'expression de sa pensée une sorte d'impressionnisme très bien noté par Lanson: 'S'il a été trop loin dans une direction, le saisissement qu'il éprouve à découvrir l'autre face des choses le jette brusquement sur le pente contraire. Sa manière d'obtenir la note moyenne, c'est de juxtaposer violemment deux tons francs.' Ce n'est pas pour lui un simple procédé de style: les notions s'offrent à lui en couples d'opposés. . . . Rousseau ne choisit pas: il accepte l'un et l'autre et, selon les cas, parlera de l'un à l'exclusion de l'autre." Pierre Burgelin, *La Philosophie de l'Existence de J.-J. Rousseau* (Paris, 1952), pp. 2–3.

ism," or to recite "the description of the Alps made by Rousseau himself" (OCs, 10:168). Although it lost this directly imitative quality, Unamuno's commitment to Rousseau continued, as may be seen in this declaration: "I have always loved Rousseau. . . . I have always loved the father of Romanticism . . . ; I have always loved this poor tormented soul who, in spite of professing, in self-defense, optimism, is the father of pessimism . . . a negator of the value of life" (EN, 2:1095–96).[2] Why Unamuno considers Rousseau a pessimist, how he altered his own response to the "maladie" of the age (the tragic sense of life) in order to benefit from Rousseau's experience with the same "illness," and why he stresses his love for Rousseau will be among the issues addressed in the following pages.

Antonio Sánchez Barbudo has done the only significant work on Unamuno's relation to Rousseau.[3] Focusing mainly on the analogy between Rousseau's Savoyard Vicar and Unamuno's San Manuel Bueno, he marks points of contact between the two men, such as the familiar problem of the identity crisis; the themes of appearance versus reality, the importance of sincerity, the need for illusion; the authors' struggles with their own ties to rationalism; their antipathy for the atheism to which they themselves contributed; and their commitment to the creative imagination. Two currents of Romanticism, both originating in Rousseau, "influence" Unamuno, Sánchez Barbudo maintains: Romanticism "à la Chateaubriand" and Romanticism "à la Sénancour." Although he refers to "influence," he concludes cautiously with the affirmation

2. The whole passage reads: "He querido siempre a Rousseau; le he querido tanto como me ha sido odioso Voltaire. He querido siempre al padre del Romanticismo, y le he querido por sus virtudes evidentes y hasta por sus más evidentes flaquezas; he querido siempre a esa pobre alma atormentada que, a pesar de profesar, por defensa propia, el optimismo, es el padre del pesimismo. Y en este punto no se para Lemaître, ni me parece haber visto bien que, a pesar de las apariencias, Rousseau, el padre espiritual de *Obermann*, fué siempre un sombrío pesimista, un negador del valor de la vida." (Cf. OCs, 3:1200–1201). Unless otherwise indicated, all translations are my own.

3. A. Sánchez Barbudo, *Estudios Sobre Unamuno y Machado* (Madrid, 1959). Sánchez Barbudo's excellent study, confirming not only the existence of the relationship between Unamuno and Rousseau but the necessity for a much broader investigation of the topic, is the point of departure for the present essay. See also Armando Zubizarreta, *Unamuno en su Nivola* (Madrid, 1960), p. 233: "Indudablemente, en la raíz de esta obra [*Como se hace una novela*] y de toda la producción Unamuniana está presente el romanticismo antropológico a la manera rousseauiana."

of "affinity" between the authors (Sánchez Barbudo, p. 82). Caution is well advised in such studies, of course, particularly when the critic is asserting the cosmopolitan origin of something that could possibly be innate in the local or national tradition. However, considering that Unamuno is "the first Spaniard to practice the literature of confession," we are justified in granting the necessity for comparing him with the modern originator of that mode.[4]

Limited mostly to the comparison of religious attitudes, Sánchez Barbudo's study suggests but does not develop another point of conjunction between these authors—the Herostratus theme. Most commentators mention Herostratus as an important factor in Unamuno's work, but Sánchez Barbudo, referring to Unamuno and Rousseau as "exhibicionistas,ególatras, destructivos y confusos," actually relates Unamuno's "erostratismo" to Rousseau's *Confessions*, a comparison which is one point of departure for the present study of Unamuno's reading of Rousseau.

This study is prompted not only by Unamuno's explicit references to Rousseau and Sánchez Barbudo's important precedent, but also by Unamuno's challenge to his colleagues to stop attributing every unknown influence in his work to Nietzsche. The professors, he states, should come up with some of his "Butlers," Samuel Butler seeming so much an echo of Unamuno's own thoughts as to suggest to him the possibility of the transmigration of souls (OCs, 11:740–41). Indeed, he experienced this intersubjective intuition more than once: "And, for my part, it occurred to me many times, upon meeting a man in a literary work, not a philosopher, not a sage or thinker, upon finding a soul, not a doctrine, to say to myself: 'But I have been this!' And I have returned to life with Pascal in his century and in his atmosphere, and I have relived with Kierkegaard in Copenhagen, and thus with many others. And is this not perhaps the supreme proof of the immortality of the soul?" (AC, p. 28).

That one can experience a sense of immortality in the act of

---

4. "La obra de Unamuno, los ensayos de Unamuno, fueron precisamente la primera confesión personal de un español ante el mundo, la incorporación española a la literatura occidental de confesión." Juan Marichal, "La Originalidad de Unamuno en la Literatura de Confesión," *La Torre* 2 (1954): 27. Cf. Carlos Blanco-Aguinaga, "Unamuno's '*yoismo*' and its Relation to Traditional Spanish *Individualism*," in *Unamuno Centennial Studies*, ed. R. Martínez-López (Austin, 1966): relates Unamuno to the European tradition, including Descartes and Rousseau.

reading is of the utmost importance to a man like Unamuno obsessed with a fear of total death.[5] In fact, for Unamuno the closest one may come to resurrection and immortality is through participation in a living literary tradition ("¿No se sentirán ellos en mí como yo me siento en ellos? Después que muera lo sabré si revivo así en otros"). Hence, far from denying a debt to his predecessors or asserting his own uniqueness at the expense of others, Unamuno takes up once more the old issues: "I do not claim any novelty for most of these fantasies, any more than I claim, of course, that other voices have not resounded before mine throwing to the winds the same complaint! But he who is able to restate the same eternal complaint, out of a different mouth, simply means that the pain persists" (ST, p. 116).

Faced with the pragmatic quality of thought in which the only new ideas to be accepted are those that least disturb the old ideas, Unamuno decides simply to repeat himself constantly, thus removing the edge of strangeness from his words: "como se sepa dar forma clásica a un disparate, pasará" (OCs, 1:619). He grants both the diachronic and synchronic modes of existence of a work of art, and of culture as a whole, but stresses the latter, convinced that "all past centuries subsist today, alive, in the twentieth century" (ST, p. 116). While life unravels before us like scenes in a film strip, the film itself "remains one and complete beyond time" (ST, p. 179), something like the "ideal order" formed by the existing monuments of art described by T. S. Eliot. The living writer must do what he can to put himself in touch with that timeless society.

The point is that for Unamuno some vital essence of the author is preserved in his books, and is revitalized in the act of reading. This encounter with being in language bears a marked resemblance to the theory of reading developed by the phenomenologically oriented "Geneva School" of critics, which includes such figures as Marcel Raymond, Albert Béguin, Georges Poulet, Jean Rousset, Jean-Pierre Richard, Jean Starobinski.[6] The kind of criticism practiced by the Genevans, as described by J. Hillis Miller, is itself a special form of the literature of meditation, of the rev-

5. On Unamuno's "ansia de inmortalidad" see, for example, Julián Marías, *Miguel de Unamuno* (Madrid, 1943), pp. 19–22.

6. See J. H. Miller, "The Geneva School," in *Modern French Criticism*, ed. J. Simon (Chicago, 1972).

erie and spiritual quest associated with Switzerland, with Rousseau, Sénancour, and Amiel. Juan Marichal lists these same three authors as determining Unamuno's spiritual destiny and his vocation as a writer of confessions.[7] In short, the experience that Unamuno had while reading Butler, Kierkegaard, and Rousseau, among others, has come to be associated with the Genevans from Rousseau to the present. A major reason for focusing on Unamuno's relation to Rousseau, then, is that, given Rousseau's status as a "privileged object" for the Geneva School, we may identify Unamuno as a "critic of consciousness" before the fact, as an important precursor of the theory of meaning developed by existential phenomenology. Indeed, works such as the study on *Don Quijote* and *Como se hace una novela* (which takes Rousseau as the model for a meditation on the mystery of the creative use of language) are significant contributions to this mode of aesthetic theory.

Unamuno anticipates[8] the modern Genevans on at least two principal points: the self-creation or discovery of the author's identity in the process of writing, and the resurrection of this paper being by others in the process of reading. Although these ideas are manifested in Unamuno's earliest works, they are most fully and explicitly elaborated in *Como se hace una novela* (1927). This book about making books opens with the author poised over the terrible whiteness of blank, Mallarméan paper, seeking to retain fleeting time, to eternalize himself. And we first see the character —U. Jugo de la Raza (Unamuno's alter ego, we are told)—at a bookstall along the Seine where he picks up a romantic autobiographical confession and begins to read. In this, his most explicit confession, his autobiography of exile, the work in which he examines his own motives, Unamuno the writer confronts himself as reader and leads us, by means of an existential treatment of the nature of literature, into a discussion of the most fundamental questions of the human condition.

Although the confessional work mentioned is identified as Balzac's *La Peau de Chagrin*, the theory expounded in *Como se hace*

7. "Rousseau, Sénancour, Amiel: esta trinidad literaria determinó el destino espiritual de Unamuno y su vocación de escritor de 'confesiones.' " Marichal, p. 25.

8. Marcel Raymond, usually said to be the founder of the Geneva School, published his important book, *De Baudelaire au surréalisme*, in 1933. See Miller, "Georges Poulet's 'Criticism of Identification,' " in *The Quest for Imagination*, ed. O. Hardison (Cleveland, 1971).

una novela owes most to Rousseau, as Unamuno explains, saying that this book is his confession "a lo Juan Jacobo" (CSH, p. 170).[9] Supporting his belief in the book as act with the example of Rousseau who "was as much responsible for the French Revolution as Mirabeau," Unamuno emphasizes the Rousseau "who spent his life explaining to us how he made the novel of his life, or rather, his representative life, which was a novel." The most profound way to live life, Unamuno concludes, is to tell about it (CSH, pp. 190, 195). He is attracted, in other words, to the Rousseau who came to think of his confessional writings as one long, unending dialog with himself, who doubled himself, becoming the author of himself as character in the *Dialogues* and his own perfect reader in the *Rêveries*.

Unamuno's understanding of these confessional writings as self-creative (as opposed to "expressionistic" theories) has become the standard theory of writing of the existential or Genevan school. Jean-Pierre Richard, for example, describes literature in general as "an exercise by which a writer both apprehends and creates himself."[10] "We are led to analyze the literary creation of Jean-Jacques as if it represented an imaginary action," Jean Starobinski similarly explains in *La Transparence et l'Obstacle*, "and his behavior as if it constituted an actually lived tale." For Starobinski, Rousseau is the exemplary embodiment of the "genetic" theory of expressive composition, the innovator of the method later adopted by surrealists of letting oneself be guided by words and emotions so that "the immediately felt reality put down on paper is the only true self." Noting this immediate contact with the self in Rousseau's writing, Maurice Blanchot makes Rousseau the watershed figure who discovers the insufficiency of traditional literature and the need to invent a new mode of writing.[11] Unfortunately, it was not within the power of Rousseau's contemporaries to discern the difference, established by the phenomenologists, between a "montreur de soi" and a "chercheur de soi."

The other key aspect of the Genevan position anticipated by

9. See the prefatory "Retrato de Unamuno" by Jean Cassou: "Hay de San Agustín en él, y de Juan Jacobo, de todos los que absortos en la contemplación de su propio milagro no pueden soportar el no ser eternos" (CSH, p. 90).

10. Sarah Lawall, *Critics of Consciousness: The Existential Structures of Literature* (Cambridge, Mass., 1968), p. 142.

11. Maurice Blanchot, *Le Livre à Venir* (Paris, 1959), p. 57.

Unamuno has to do with the ontology of the text. When T. S. Eliot, for example, proposes that the artist be set among the dead for contrast and comparison so that he, the critic, may see how the ideal order among them might be modified, or when, in stressing the interdependence of originality and tradition, he claims that the most "individual" parts of the poet's work may be those in which the dead poets, his ancestors, assert their immortality most vigorously, he is speaking about tradition impersonally, as a formalist. His description of the critical activity is accurate but gives no hint of what happens to the reader making these comparisons. The existential critics, however, absorb and extend Eliot's idea of tradition, and are more sensitive to the reader who brings the dead author's spirit to life in the work.

The issue of life and death involved in the existential experience of reading has been described pejoratively by Jean-Paul Sartre, but in a way which gives a good idea of what is at stake. Living in his library as in a cemetery, among "little coffins stacked on shelves along the walls like urns in a columbarium," the critic, Sartre says sarcastically, practices that "strange operation which he has decided to call reading: from one point of view it is a possession; he lends his body to the dead in order that they may come back to life. And from another point of view it is a contact with the beyond. Indeed, the book is by no means an object; neither is it an act, nor even a thought. Written by a dead man about dead things it no longer has any place on this earth; it speaks of nothing which interests us directly. Left to itself, it falls back and collapses; there remain only ink spots on musty paper. And when the critic reanimates these spots when he makes letters and words of them, they speak to him of passions which he does not feel, of bursts of anger without objects, of dead fears and hopes. . . . And during the time he is reading, his everyday life becomes an appearance."[12] Unlike Unamuno, Sartre extends the logic of his atheism to include the rejection of literary immortality which Unamuno believes may be attained in intersubjectivity.

Georges Poulet, on the other hand, working in the Genevan tradition, puts the phenomenology of the text into a positive context. It is true, he says, that books, those unique "objects," wait for the reader to come like an Aladdin to deliver them from their

12. Sartre, *Essays in Existentialism*, ed. Wade Baskin (New York, 1970), pp. 325–26.

immobility; they wait not like vampires, the undead, to suck away the reader's life, but rather like pets in a store window awaiting an owner, appealing mournfully to each passerby.[13] Such an appeal is a central event in *Como se hace una novela*. We cannot resist the mute appeal of the book because, Poulet says, although reading is necessarily an alienating, schizoid experience, it accomplishes nothing less than the salvation of an author's identity from death. The salvation occurs during reading when "a work of literature becomes, at the expense of the reader whose own life it suspends, a sort of human being, a mind conscious of itself and constituting itself in me as the subject of its own objects."[14]

This resurrection of the author's consciousness is at the heart of Unamuno's theory of tradition. It is the rationale for his blending of literature and philosophy, for his stance as a commentator not only on the books of others, but on his own. In *Como se hace una novela*, Jugo de la Raza at first resists reading, fearing a vertiginous loss of self, a fear of death, which Unamuno counteracts in his commentary by reminding the reader that reading must not be passive, that it is a living re-creation. Properly understood it is a way not to lose, but to find oneself. Following the phenomenological theory that consciousness is always an "intentionality," that it grasps itself through being conscious of something other than itself, both Poulet and Unamuno insist on the co-presence of author and reader during reading. "When you make yourself reader, make yourself author or rather, actor, at the same time," Unamuno says, speaking to the reader from the author's point of view. The result is an interpenetration of reader and author in which Unamuno's "intraman" unites with the reader's "intraman," "in such a way that I live in you and you in me" (CSH, p. 186). "I am not victimized by the other's possession of my consciousness," Poulet as reader agrees, "rather I share the use of my consciousness with this being at the heart of the book whom I am trying to define": "Lui et moi, nous nous mettons à avoir une conscience mitoyenne" (*Critique*, p. 285). The extraordinary thing about reading, Poulet says, "is that between you and the book the barriers fall. You are in it, and it is in you, there is no longer an outside

13. Poulet, *La Conscience Critique* (Paris, 1971), p. 275.
14. Poulet, "Criticism and the Experience of Interiority," in *The Languages of Criticism and the Sciences of Man*, eds. Macksey and Donato (Baltimore, 1970), pp. 61, 32.

or inside" (*Critique*, p. 217). This transcendence of the old dualism by entering the mental world of books is what Unamuno is referring to in his enigmatic, oft-repeated paradox that "the noumenal invented by Kant is the most phenomenal thing there is, and substance the most formal. *El fondo de una cosa es superficie*" (CSH, p. 171).

The only difference between the creative critic Poulet and the philosopher-novelist Unamuno regarding this triumph over dualism in the union of reader and writer stems from their different orientations: as critic, Poulet is more concerned about the reception of thought; as novelist, Unamuno is concerned about projecting his thought. Thus, whereas Unamuno seeks inclusion in a tradition as a means to *personal* salvation, Poulet lends his consciousness to dead authors in a disinterested way, free, Hillis Miller says, of "Promethean" motives. Nonetheless, in taking as his central critical motif the existentialist theme of man's desire to be like God, Poulet is searching in the works of other authors for answers to personal questions, questions very similar to those which obsess Unamuno.[15] In short, the phenomenology of reading is in part a metaphysical exercise. "In our sacred imagination," Unamuno explains, "which fuses centuries and vast territories, which makes time into eternity and space into infinity," the reader and author enjoy "a mutual salvation" (CSH, pp. 153, 205). Eternal life depends exclusively "en alimentarse de las demás individuales y darse a ellas en alimento" (CSH, pp. 115–16). Thus the search for oneself in language that a Rousseau initiates, Unamuno says, does not end with death "because his intimate, internalized, novelistic life continues in the life of his readers" (CSH, p. 192). This continuation, the uninterrupted flow of spiritual nourishment carried in books from generation to generation, is tradition. The typical appeal of the misunderstood romantic genius to posterity has for Unamuno a religious connotation: reading is an act of grace.

Whatever the differences between their ambitions as writers, Poulet and Unamuno as readers are exactly alike, sharing an intense interest in Rousseau as the first in a line of romantic authors who created in his reveries "a human equivalent of the divine *totum simul.*"[16] Rousseau's imitation of immortality, his achieve-

15. Hardison, pp. 192, 208.
16. Ibid.

ment of self-presence, makes him the protagonist of the phenomenological approach to literature. Of course the "cogito" or
essence of the author sought by Poulet in his reading is not the
historical man but an autonomous identity, the virtual self created in language. Nor does Unamuno, as much as he desires a "personal" immortality, deceive himself on this point. In fact, he anticipates the objection to Poulet made by René Girard that the
reader does not identify himself with the "cogito" any more than
with the historical man but with the character.[17] It is not Cervantes
but Don Quixote who lives and thrives in the minds of successive
generations of readers, creating for himself a certain independence
out of this plurality, Unamuno says. "And my Augusto Pérez
[protagonist of *Niebla*] was no doubt right to tell me . . . that perhaps I was nothing but a pretext so that his story and the stories
of others, including my own, could come into the world" (TNE,
p. 13). The point is that the historical man has no essential identity to transfer into the work, but invents it as he goes along
(existence precedes essence). Unamuno, in short, professes an existentialist modification of the romantic or expressionist aesthetics
held by Rousseau, a modification that reverses the relation between identity and expression. Some of the consequences of this
reversal as it affects the theme of the author's legend will be outlined in the following chapters.

———

Since Unamuno's day there have been certain refinements in our
understanding of how a tradition is constituted, refinements which
have had an impact on the methodology of comparative literature. The "crisis in comparative literature" to which René Wellek
addressed himself at the 1958 International Congress involved a
methodological reorientation away from the so-called Paris
School of comparatists, with its restrictive, historical approach,
to a liberalized understanding of literary relations intended to
bring comparatists closer to the aesthetic object.[18] It is clear now
that the proliferation of articles on influence study that appeared
throughout the 1950s involved a readjustment which brought

17. Macksey, p. 82.
18. See Harry Levin, *Grounds for Comparison* (Cambridge, Mass., 1972), pp.
84–85.

comparatism into line with the lessons of formalist aesthetics. In fact, the readjustment was so complete that a term other than "influence" was needed to describe the study of literary indebtedness (a principal interest of comparative literature), particularly in so far as this study dealt with textual similarities.

Agreeing that the old positivistic, extrinsic approach to influence is inadequate, the leading comparatists—Harry Levin, A. Owen Aldridge, Ihab Hassan, Haskell Block, and Claudio Guillén, to name a few—all suggest that the concept of "tradition" better reflects the new orientation.[19] My purpose, therefore, as a part of this introduction to a study of a tradition, is to examine the methodological implications of this concept, to review the status of *tradition* as a critical term, in order to describe one of the more meaningful modes of access to the relations that exist between two authors.

What is needed is a methodology that permits an adequate discussion of literary indebtedness while avoiding the extremes of positivism, which has too much methodology, and impressionism, which has too little. Hassan, in an article appearing in 1955, outlined the terms for such a method. To deal with literary relations in the broadest possible context, Hassan replaces the two primary components of influence—similarity and causality—with the notions of tradition and development respectively. He likes Heinrich Wölfflin's definition of traditions as distinct structural patterns, as sets of norms both of language and attitude, unrestricted to any epoch. And development, he explains, is simply the modification of one tradition into another, viewed always in terms of historical perspectivism—understanding the past in terms of the present. Not the vain study of "sources" and influences, but the definition of the poet's type through direct comparisons with manifestations of the same type in other languages and periods is what Hassan, paraphrasing T. S. Eliot, demands.

19. Aldridge, ed. *Comparative Literature: Matter and Method* (Urbana, 1969), pp. 1–5; Aldridge, et al., "The Concept of Influence in Comparative Literature," *CLS* (Special Introductory Issue); Anna Balakian, "Influence and Literary Fortune: The Equivocal Junction of Two Methods," *YCGL* 11 (1962); Block, "The Concept of Influence in Comparative Literature," *YCGL* 7 (1958); Hassan, "The Problem of Influence in Literary History," *JAAC* 14 (1955); Ulrich Weisstein, *Comparative Literature and Literary Theory*, trans. W. Riggan (Bloomington, Ind., 1973); René Wellek, "The Name and Nature of Comparative Literature," in *Comparatists at Work*, ed. Stephen Nichols and R. Vowles (Waltham, Mass., 1968).

Hassan's explicit attempt to place influence study in the context of a systematic view of literature prepares the way for an appreciation of Guillén, whose 1957 essay "Literatura como sistema" outlines a methodology adequate to the task of synthesis proposed by Hassan and the other comparatists who advocate the shift from influence to tradition.[20] By giving primary attention to the aesthetic object without falling into the trap of a random notation of affinities, Guillén's application of Ferdinand Saussure's structural linguistics to influence study solves the main problems associated with the formalist reorientation of comparatism.

Saussure, as is now well known, by separating *langue* from *parole*, was able to treat language scientifically, a split that has its equivalent in the formalist's separation of the work from its author. *Langue*, the systematic level, refers to the social aspect of language which is not complete in any speaker, but exists perfectly only within the collectivity; *parole* refers to the individual utterance which activates the system. For Guillén, the totality of written texts is the dictionary of literature activated or given utterance by the reader.

Although language changes and evolves, that is, exists diachronically, it exists synchronically as a whole in the present of any one speaker. An analogy sometimes used to describe the unity which a synchronic viewpoint brings to language is that of a landscape perspective: what you see depends on your position, but your point of view always gives unity to the scene.[21] Similarly, out of the chaos of relational possibilities in the whole of literature, Guillén maintains, the specific associations that take place in the cultured reader's mind make up the groupings that he calls "living" traditions.

To explain how transformations occur within the system, Guillén draws upon the formalist theory of development in literary history. Boris Eichenbaum provided a convenient summation of the Russian formalist aesthetic which maintains, apropos of Guillén's position, that no amount of genetic study could illuminate

20. In *Filología Romanza* 4 (1957): 1–29. Cf. "The Aesthetics of Influence Studies in Comparative Literature," in *Proceedings of the Second Congress of the International Comparative Literature Association,* ed. W. Friedrich (Chapel Hill, N.C., 1958), pp. 176–92; and *Literature as System* (Princeton, 1971).

21. Frederick A. Pottle, "Synchrony and Diachrony: A Plea for the Use in Literary Studies of Saussure's Concepts and Terminology," in *Literary Theory and Structure,* ed. Brady and Palmer (New Haven, 1973), p. 8.

the literariness of literature.[22] Insisting on the autonomy of literature, Eichenbaum declared the chief influence on a work of literature to be other literary works. Literature evolves, according to this view, by means of a dialectical argument called defamiliarization. In the same vein, Roman Jakobson, who is usually credited with uniting linguistics and formalist poetics, says that a work has meaning only in terms of the literary system in which it fits.[23] Through him it was seen that change is itself a synchronic phenomenon directly experienced by the reader.[24] In the reader's consciousness, synchrony and diachrony interpenetrate; the reader, as Eliot would agree, appreciates novelty in terms of the traditional and conventional context.

Guillén, taking up these linguistic and aesthetic concepts in the context of influence study, sets out to discover how far comparatists actually apply the comparative method, for comparison, more than a method, *is an aesthetic experience.* Guillén justifies the formalist exclusion of genetic issues by distinguishing what he calls "influence"—a psychological issue having to do with the creative process occurring in the author's mind—from "tradition" —objectively observable textual relations. Textual similarities and the fact of influence, he stresses, are unrelated, an insight which is the basis of "intertextuality." Literary relationships, he says, *belong to the reader's experience,* are aesthetic facts. Whereas Eliot put the author at the center of tradition, Guillén, following the lead of Jakobson, defines tradition in terms of the reader. Tradition is *the whole of the possible textual relations latent in literature to which the reader may give life.*

We are prepared now to appreciate the practical implications for our study in Guillén's closing remarks. "The comparatist, more than anyone else," he states, "must demonstrate to what extent the aesthetic experience attracts and articulates entire combinations of artistic creations, not only because these conjunctions justify the comparative method, but because without it there would be no such conjunctions." The synchronic comparatist, in short, must set aside genetic issues, historical positivism, and con-

22. "The Theory of the 'Formal Method,'" in *Russian Formalist Criticism,* trans. Lee Lemon and Marion Reis (Lincoln, Neb., 1965).
23. "Linguistics and Poetics," in *The Structuralists from Marx to Lévi-Strauss,* ed. R. and F. DeGeorge (New York, 1972).
24. R. Scholes, *Structuralism in Literature* (New Haven, 1974), p. 90.

centrate upon a direct confrontation of texts. If the comparatist's interest is the Rousseau tradition in Unamuno, the proper question to ask is not whether the historical Unamuno read *Emile*, although such information should be used where it exists, but how the present reader, with *Emile* in mind, might respond to *Amor y Pedagogía*, for example; or vice versa!

Regarding this latter possibility, the reversibility of the experience, Guillén's method allows the comparatist to make more than random use of Eliot's insight into the simultaneous, extratemporal interaction of works with radically different contexts. To support the point that later works in a tradition modify our appreciation of earlier ones, Guillén draws upon his Spanish background as well as upon Eliot, citing the ideas of Pedro Salinas, Ortega y Gasset, and, significantly, the "eternal tradition" of *En torno al casticismo* by Unamuno himself. Thus it happens that the Herostratus factor in Rousseau's thinking is heightened and made visible by the juxtaposition with Unamuno. Some of Guillén's examples of tradition include the way Proust modifies our appreciation of Henry James, Malraux, and Chateaubriand, and the way a familiarity with the "enigma of the personality" presented in Dostoevsky affects our reading of Balzac, Stendhal, or Turgenev, making us more sensitive to the distinct resolutions these authors offer to the same enigma. "Whenever we read with artistic taste a great writer," Guillén says, "a series of living traditions arrange themselves around him. And there are as many arrangements of this type as there are works capable of sustaining them." The conclusion of the sentence contains the key to the method. Such conjunctions become traditions worthy of a place in literary history when they can sustain the full activation or utterance that results from a critical or "systematic" investigation of the original aesthetic experience.

Nor does the method of synchronic comparatism impose on Unamuno's own sensibility, for he self-consciously works by a dialog or argument with the great figures of literature and philosophy, performing thus a certain defamiliarization or "swerve" on the tradition just as the formalists describe it. There is, in fact, a notable methodological similarity between the reader orientation of Guillén's structuralist approach and the phenomenological approach of the Genevans. The most recent contribution to the theory of tradition we have been discussing does indeed seem to unify these two methodological approaches—intersubjectivity and intertextuality, influence and tradition—that contribution being Harold Bloom's theory of antithetical criticism. Although he focuses primarily on what Guillén calls "influence"—the psychological phenomenon which is part of the creative process, not of the text—Bloom approaches the question of literary relations in the terms stated at the beginning of this study, that is, by considering poets as readers first, readers in defensive, aggressive or sympathetic dialog with their antecedents. He adds that the critic, too, is a creative writer who, in seeking his own place in the library of Babel, practices a form of creative misreading.

The following chapters, then, present an investigation based on aesthetic comparatism and, if Bloom is right, perhaps on antithetical criticism as well.[25] It is in any case an imaginative vivification of a latent tradition, in Guillén's sense of the term, although the obvious historical or biographical data relating the flesh and blood Unamuno to Rousseau are included also. Our discussion of Rousseau, therefore, will be guided by Unamuno's point of view, the point being to reconstruct Unamuno's reading of Rousseau. While realizing the connection in my mind, it seemed to me that the relationship has to be dramatized, that the critic has a creative responsibility to his materials, if only to the extent of showing how Unamuno, confronted with the Herostratus factor in existence, may have benefited from Rousseau's struggle with a similar condition.[26] The drama exists latently, metaphorically, in the volumes as they lie open side by side on the desk, depending upon the scholar's "competence" for its realization, which is the way traditions are made, and authors immortalized.

25. Bloom's works, especially *The Anxiety of Influence* and *The Map of Misreading*, prove that when a mode of inquiry seems exhausted, as was the case with influence study, it may only be catching its breath.

26. As one handbook states it, "The active attempt to master the past, to see it in terms of the present, to solve present problems in line with the solutions and achievements of the past—these make the writer 'traditional' in the best sense." Joseph Shipley, ed., *Dictionary of World Literature* (Totowa, N.J., 1968), p. 419.

1. The Legend of Herostratus

The aspiring youth that fired the Ephesian dome
Outlives the pious fool that raised it.
COLLEY CIBBER (1671–1757)

In the year 356 B.C., the temple of Artemis at Ephesus, remarkable for its great size and for the art with which it was adorned, one of the seven wonders of the ancient world, was destroyed by fire. It is said that Herostratus, a man about whom nothing else is known, committed the act so that his name might live forever in the memories of men. In spite of a decree that it not be mentioned, on pain of death, the name survives, however marginally, in our awareness, outlasting all but one of the seven wonders and as durable as the pyramids themselves. If the legend has survived it is because it tells us something about human nature, which is why Miguel de Unamuno adopted and developed the legend as an existential emblem. The key to the modern applicability of the Herostratus factor, as we shall see in our discussion of two authors whose works bear the mark of Herostratus, is the translation of reputation (fame) into identity. In the modern crisis of self, any identity will do so long as it can be determined that it is our identity, hence that selfhood is possible, just as for Herostratus any reputation would do so long as he had one.

To a certain extent all ancient art is a response to a desire for fame, Arnold Hauser reminds us, the wish to be renowned in the eyes of contemporaries and posterity, with the story of Herostratus serving as evidence of the undiminished power of this passion into the later Hellenistic period.[1] But why should the desire

1. Hauser, *The Social History of Art*, vol. 1 (New York, 1951), p. 59.

17

for recognition be associated with such a destructive crime? Is Herostratus, who listened all his life to heroic lays in which a noble was glorified for feats of destruction in war, perhaps the first recorded example, considering his confusion of fame and notoriety, of an unbalanced individual adversely affected by the media? The clue to the meaning of the legend, a clue which Unamuno must have known about, is the association of the birth of Alexander the Great with the firing of the temple. The two events, Plato says, took place on the same night.[2] We may infer from this juxtaposition that it was not a positive desire for glory that moved Herostratus—the usual explanation of his motive—but, as Unamuno asserts, an overwhelmingly negative emotion—envy—directed at Alexander. Arson, moreover, in its pure destructiveness, is a crime frequently motivated by envy.[3]

We may imagine, then, that on that evening in 356 B.C., as Herostratus passed by the familiar temple, runners from the court of Philip of Macedon were announcing the birth of the prince for whom great things were prophesied. The thought of this child, born into all the advantages of life and predestined for glory, made Herostratus reflect despairingly on his own frustrated ambitions, made him rage against his anonymity, mortality, mediocrity. So, after sharing in the many jugs of wine passed about amongst the revelers toasting the King's good fortune, Herostratus took a torch from a passing procession and went into the temple, there to light a fire which is the image of the passion of envy, as well as of fame.

Herostratus has not been forgotten because his action is a manifestation of what it is to be a human being. His example provides a point of reference for our own insight into the special affinity of thought that exists between Unamuno and Rousseau. Before examining this affinity, however, we should first consider the context of our reference point—the qualities that have been associated with Herostratus over the centuries—so that we may appreciate Unamuno's view of the herostratic aspect of existence.

We may begin with the Renaissance, a time when, along with other attributes of antiquity, the cult of fame was rekindled in

2. Recorded in *Timaeus.* See F. Noël, *Dictionnaire de la Fable,* vol. 1 (Paris, 1810).

3. Helmut Schoeck, *Envy: A Theory of Social Behaviour,* trans. M. Glenny and B. Ross (New York, 1969), p. 119. Although this study is wide-ranging, it makes no mention of Rousseau or Unamuno.

the minds of men. Commenting on the relation of the thirst for fame to the birth of individualism in the Italian Renaissance, Jacob Burckhardt records two points that bear directly on our theme. In the first place, steeped as they were in Roman authors who were themselves obsessed with the conception of fame, and finding themselves in an atmosphere in which poets were being revered in a way formerly reserved for saints, Renaissance men of letters displayed a boundless ambition that used any means, including infamous deeds, to attain distinction. "These are characteristic features of an age of highly excited but already despairing passions and forces," Burckhardt writes, "*and remind us of the burning of the temple at Ephesus in the time of Philip of Macedon.*"[4] Glory and notoriety, barely distinguished in our culture, were already merging in the Renaissance. The second point, especially significant for the understanding of our authors' formulations of the problem, is Burckhardt's comment, accounting for the rise of wit and satire in Renaissance literature, that "the corrective, not only of fame and the modern desire for fame but of all highly developed individuality, is *ridicule and scorn. . . .*" Consequently a large brood of wits, critics, and railers grew up *whose envy*, Burckhardt says, required "hecatomes of victims." We shall see that the envy which motivates the desire for fame is experienced as a painful sense of being ridiculous oneself, for, as Socrates notes in *Philebus*, the laughter involved with the ridicule of others is envious: our pleasure in the misfortune of others is caused by envy, a painful sensation, so that our mocking laughter is bittersweet at best.[5] Because it had so many suitable individualists as targets, Renaissance Florence was a greater "school for scandal" even than Voltaire's France, according to Burckhardt. Helmut Schoeck, on the other hand, feels that envious intrigue, at least among literati, was strongest in eighteenth-century France.[6]

4. *The Civilization of the Renaissance in Italy* (New York, 1961), p. 134, my italics. Cf. Erwin Panofsky, *Meaning in the Visual Arts* (Garden City, N.Y., 1955), p. 137: "The great man of the Renaissance asserted his personality centripetally, so to speak: he swallowed up the world that surrounded him until his whole environment had been absorbed by his own self. [Abbot] Suger asserted his personality centrifugally: he projected his ego into the world that surrounded him until his whole self had been absorbed by his environment"—which is to say that Suger was still a medieval man.

5. G. B. Milner, "Homo Ridens," *Semiotica* 5–6 (1972): 4.

6. Schoeck, p. 156.

Recalling in this regard the opening of Rousseau's *Confessions*, which is a manifesto of that individualism born in the Renaissance ("But I am made unlike any one I have ever met; I will even venture to say that I am like no one in the whole world. I may be no better, but at least I am different"), it is easy to understand why Rousseau received so much attention from the envious mockers who made up the "conspiracy" which he imagined had been formed to defame him. Unamuno, of course, made similar statements: "There is no other me. There may be greater and lesser, better and worse, but there is no other me. I am something entirely new" (DQ, p. 211). We need to remember here that, as we shall see, the original motive for the individualism which attracts envious ridicule is envy itself. Rousseau and Unamuno begin as enviers, but by their actions show that it is no better to be the envied than the envier.

While on the secular side of the Renaissance individualism and envy, fame and ridicule, developed together, even becoming interdependent, there was also a religious source for their conjunction; but the immortality sought in the latter case represented a desire to *escape* the envious agony experienced in the pursuit of fame. The tradition involved is that of the holy fool, or wise fool, many aspects of which parallel the strategies and attitudes of the authors to be discussed. Our authors' strategies to avoid envy by imitating God, for example, may be linked in spirit to the *Imitatio Christi* by Thomas à Kempis and *De docta ignorantia* by Nicholas of Cusa, medieval works upon which Erasmus drew for his creation of the first protagonist fool of the Renaissance.[7] The effort to live like God while still on earth among men, and hence to be worthy of immortality, obviously makes a man appear ridiculous to his secularized contemporaries.

Like Rousseau, who upheld the paradox that progress in the arts and sciences caused man's degeneration, the fool in Christ, following the various dictates in the Gospels and in St. Paul, opposed "Scholastic" learning and exalted the simple life of Jesus as a model for earthly conduct. For his trouble, or because of what might be called his "alienation," the fool, it was believed, received the special protection of God. Not only was the fool the

7. Walter Kaiser, *Praisers of Folly: Erasmus, Rabelais, Shakespeare* (Cambridge, Mass., 1963). I am indebted in these pages to Kaiser's discussion of the tradition of the wise fool.

champion of the heart against the head or rationality, but also, in the ancient argument between nature and law (custom), the fool lived by the "law" of nature. With the license his eccentricity afforded him he could become an iconoclastic force, he could cut through euphemisms and obfuscations and speak the truth. Rousseau, with his appeals for "transparency" and his belief that man is innocent and society corrupt, borrows directly from this tradition, representing what Walter Kaiser calls the "fool of nature."

The "ridiculous appearance" typical of the wise fool is traditionally exemplified in Alcibiades' comparison of Socrates to a grotesque Silenus image which, when opened, reveals a god's icon. The literary device equivalent to this mask used by the praisers of folly to revaluate values is given its "classic formulation," Kaiser says, by Sebastien Chamfort, who observed that to have a just idea of things one must take words in the opposite sense from that given them by the world (Kaiser, p. 54). As much mocked as mocker, the fool depends on irony, on the equipoise of jest and earnest, to protect himself in his gadfly role, and paradox is one of the best means to achieve the needed balance. Defining paradox as the "divine language" consisting of a "desvía de común sentir" (AP, p. 279), Unamuno consistently practices the fool's inversions. "Take the opposite of common usage," Rousseau advises similarly, "and you will almost always do well" (E, p. 83). As an example of the universality of inversion as a way to wisdom there is the Sioux heyoka ceremony in which everything is done backwards to make the people laugh. Truth has two faces, the medicine man Black Elk says, one is sad, one laughs. In time of despair the clown is the best medium of the sacred power.[8]

The fool's purpose in turning the world upside down is to undermine all complacency, but the result may be either comic or tragic or, more often, tragicomic. In fact, the association of the fool with tragedy, exemplified by Hamlet, who is a fool transfigured, according to Gilbert Murray, is essential to the hero-

8. John G. Neihardt, *Black Elk Speaks* (Lincoln, Neb., 1961), pp. 192–94. "The mainspring of tragedy-as-spectacle," Roland Barthes notes, "is the same as that of any providential metaphysics: reversal. To change all things into their opposite is both the formula of divine power and the very recipe of tragedy." *On Racine* (New York, 1964), p. 41. Reversal is also the recipe of comedy. On the relations of tragic and comic formulas see Marie C. Swabey, *Comic Laughter* (New Haven, 1961), pp. 180–85; J. L. Styan, *The Dark Comedy* (Cambridge, England, 1962), pp. 35–41.

stratic world view. Another such figure is Don Quixote, the figure who closed the Renaissance tradition of the wise fool with a touch of tragedy. Don Quixote, of course, provides the key to Unamuno's place in this larger context. Those aspects of *Don Quijote* which Unamuno singles out as the points of departure for his tragicomic sense of life are exactly the features that prompted Kaiser to include the work in his *Praisers of Folly*. It is, for example, the most ironic story ever told, Kaiser says, making what is jest indistinguishable from what is serious. He also points out the same warning to mockers used by Unamuno: for taking such pains to mock a fool, the Duke and Duchess are themselves made ridiculous. "Like all fools," Kaiser says, Don Quixote lives in an upside-down world, "al revés," has the capacity to see himself from the point of view of others, and confuses illusion and reality. But in Don Quixote's case the secular and holy fools are mixed—the desire for immortality manifests itself as a quest for fame, indicating that the goal of the two kinds of fool is the same: to make it possible to live with the tragic quality of life. A standard part of the fool's inversion of values important to our authors is the praise of self-love against the grain of the Christian virtue of self-hate, an inversion which was justified in the Renaissance by reasoning that to be able to love his neighbor a man must first love himself (Kaiser, p. 68). Both Rousseau and Unamuno insist that their self-love is altruistic in exactly this sense. Their subjective, self-directed approach to an understanding of the human condition, however immodest it may seem, is an axiom of existential practice. "I can question myself," Sartre says, for example, "and on the basis of this interrogation, successfully carry out an analysis of human reality which will serve as a formulation for an anthropology."[9] In Erasmian terms, the point the fool wants to make by flaunting the foolishness he discovers in himself is that, at base, all men are fools (Kaiser, p. 14). The comic laugh eases the pain of the tragic recognition, which is why our authors want to place themselves in the tradition of the fool.

Exemplifying the consequences of the individualism inherent in Christianity, the authors' specific mode of exhibitionism—their self-ridicule, which places them in the tradition of the fool—retains enough of the self-mortification of the religious confession

9. Quoted by E. W. Knight, in *Literature Considered as Philosophy* (New York, 1962), pp. 107–8.

to mark it as an act of righteous and therefore fundamentally orthodox Christian pride. But there is nothing like righteousness to generate misunderstanding and hostility in a secularized community. As Rousseau admits, he was out of place in the Parisian salon, the atmosphere of which might have recalled the easygoing contempt for everyone and everything that was the prevailing tone in Florentine Renaissance society. But Unamuno's response to his envious community—his invention of the self as a spectacle —was exactly what Burckhardt says worked best in calumnious Florence, that is, apparent contempt for all accusations accompanied by "joyous display." Rousseau's protestation of innocence, on the other hand, in a situation similar to that in Florence where claims of virtue were the surest way to arouse attacks of malice, was clearly a poor strategy for turning aside envy.

We shall see, finally, that the authors' individualism, their self-love, is an interesting form of envy-avoidance, a mode of conduct fundamental to the socialization of man. By declaring themselves to be "incomparable," an action which attracts the ridicule of the railers, they are repressing their own envy, envy being a passion which originates in the comparison of oneself to the other. They are less concerned with being envied, however, than with suffering themselves the agony of envying others, although envy-avoidance more commonly refers to the avoidance of *being* envied.

Marking the transition from a religious to a secular world view in the Renaissance, then, there were two classes of "ridiculous" men to which the envious mockers could give their attention—the holy fools seeking immortality, and the new individualists seeking fame. That the two sorts were often confused is suggested by the fate of Rousseau, who clearly thought of himself as a holy fool, as a Don Quixote, but whose life was interpreted in terms of secular egotism. As we enter the modern age with its psychological sophistication (Rousseau being perhaps *the* transitional figure), it becomes less important to distinguish the two modes. We now know that egotism and martyrdom are not incompatible.

Fame and immortality, envy and ridicule: here are the ingredients of the legend of Herostratus which Unamuno turns into an "ism"—"erostratismo"—signifying a mode of being that is the key to his interest in Rousseau. Let us consider, now, what the legend means to Unamuno, and how Rousseau becomes involved with it.

The "illness of the age," defined as the loss of faith in the existence of God, originated, according to Unamuno, with Rousseau (ST, p. 261). Being sick to death with this illness caused Unamuno to meditate at length upon the example of one of the first men to intuit it, and upon the example of Herostratus whose legend symbolizes the tragic sense of life. Unamuno openly declares the connection between the tragic sense of life and herostratism: "Tremendous passion, this, that our memory survive in spite of the forgetfulness of others if it is possible. From it arises envy. . . . And this herostratism, what is it, at base, but desire for immortality, even if not of substance and bulk, at least of name and shadow?" (ST, p. 54). He notes that he is touched with the same "locura de no morir" that motivated Don Quixote's ambivalent disquisition on fame, which is itself based on the Herostratus legend (in *Don Quijote* 2.1).

As developed by Unamuno, "erostratismo" represents a feeling described as an obsession with self-expansion: "More, more, and each time more," Unamuno says; "I want to be myself, and, without ceasing to be myself, to be at the same time the others, to internalize the totality of things visible and invisible, to extend myself to the boundlessness of space and prolong myself to the endlessness of time" (ST, pp. 39–40). "Nor is this pride," he adds, "but terror of the void. We try to be all, seeing in it the only way to avoid being reduced to nothing. We want to save our memory, at least our memory" (ST, p. 55). Such an aggressive passion is the consequence of the death of God, of the demystification of religion by science which gives rise to a terrible contradiction, to a "perpetual battle between the head and the heart, reason and feeling, without victory or hope of victory" (ST, p. 38), that is, to the tragic sense of life. In Unamuno's experience of this sense, then, the drives of the fool (who favors the heart) and of the literatus (who favors the head) are combined.

Rousseau's special contribution to the tragic sentiment is precisely this concern for both a worldly and an extra-worldly immortality—he wants the love of man as well as the love of God. What Unamuno responds to, then, is Rousseau's mixture of religious fervor with social psychology, a mixture in which Unamuno is able to "relive" all his own opinions. The basis of relationships among people in society, both authors believe, is envy. The formulating act of civilization is the act of comparison. For Unamuno the point is perfectly represented in the story of Cain and Abel: "And Cain killed Abel because of envy," and in the city founded by Cain civilization began (O, p. 57). As for Rousseau, it could be said that his entire explanation of the origin of inequality is an account of the evolution of what Unamuno calls herostratism: "Each one began to look at the others and to want to be looked at himself, and public esteem had a value. . . . And this was the first step towards inequality, and towards vice at the same time . . ." (CS, p. 71). The consequences of that first comparison were terrible and may be surmised from Rousseau's cry, "O fury to distinguish oneself, what will you not do!" Man began to measure offenses or slights according to the degree he felt his own self-esteem compromised, rather than according to the actual harm done, and hence acts of revenge became frightful, and man turned cruel and bloodthirsty. "Mépris" became the worst of all offenses as man learned for the first time what it was to feel like a fool.

Here Unamuno would take special notice, for the goal of this fury to distinguish oneself, Rousseau says, is immortality. The desire for "réputation" makes civilized man work "to the point of death, he runs to it even in order to put himself in a position to live, *or renounces life in order to acquire immortality*" (CS, pp. 91–92, my italics). Social man, as opposed to natural man, lives not inside, but outside himself, in the opinion of others, "and, as it were, takes solely from their judgment the sense of his own existence." Produced by the comparative amour-propre which Rousseau calls "the negative sensibility," the socializing impulse manifests itself as the desire to be all: "Because as soon as one gets into the habit of measuring oneself with others . . . it is impossible to not take an aversion to everything that surpasses us, everything that lowers us, everything that restrains us, everything that, being something, prevents us from being all" (D, p. 149). This negative will, identified later by Unamuno as the herostratic urge, is the basic passion of man in society, according to Rousseau: "After having swallowed many treasures and desolated many men, my hero will finish by slaughtering everything until he is the sole master of the universe. Such briefly is the moral tableau, if not of human life, at least of the secret pretensions in the heart of every civilized man" (CS, p. 102). Reading these lines by Rousseau Unamuno must cry out, "¡Pero este he sido yo!" for in them he finds an exact description of his own deepest anguish, of the "congoja" of the tragic sense.

But having recognized himself in Rousseau's social man, Unamuno penetrates Rousseau's intentions to identify Rousseau himself with this herostratic urge to distinguish oneself. Consider, for example, this passage from *Emile* quoted in *Del Sentimiento Trágico de la Vida*: " 'Each one knows that his system is no better established than the others, but he defends it because it is his. . . . Where is one who in the recesses of his heart proposes anything other than to distinguish himself? . . . The essential thing is to think differently from the others.' How much truth there is in the profundity of these sad confessions by that man of painful sincerity!" (ST, p. 52). This passage is a major clue in determining how Unamuno read Rousseau. Unamuno implies that Rousseau is here confessing his own "sin," one that Unamuno obviously recognizes as his own, when in context (the passage is from the "Profession de Foi"), Rousseau is *attacking* the philosophers and literati while claiming that he himself has no such pretensions. Unamuno clearly does not believe these claims, but he understands why they were made. We must remember, however, that when Unamuno looks into Rousseau's soul he discovers not only the first and most thorough description of that condition called herostratism but also an intense disgust with it. In the next chapter we shall consider both Rousseau's participation in and opposition to herostratism, along with Unamuno's views of Rousseau as herostratic man.

2. The New Herostratus?

*I was reluctant to leave my fellow men
before they had learnt my true worth,
before they knew how deserving I
should have appeared of their love if
they had known me better*

J.-J. ROUSSEAU

One of the most controversial figures in all of literary or intellectual history, Rousseau had the problem, not of being
forgotten, but of being remembered as someone he himself would
recognize, which is the problem of the legend. From the time of
his break with the *philosophes* and the condemnation of his works
by Parliament, the Sorbonne, the Archbishop of Paris, and the
authorities of Berne, Neuchâtel and Holland, up to Unamuno's
own day (with the exception of the Revolutionary period), Rousseau's reputation has been assailed ceaselessly.[1] Blamed for
everything from libertinism to totalitarianism, Rousseau in every
period met those who would call him "monster," a "soul gnawed
by vice on the blanched sepulcher of ostentation."[2]

Pierre Lasserre began the assault in Unamuno's time, during the
bicentenary commemoration of Rousseau's birth, finding in Rousseau the source of a sickness infecting the sensibility, intelligence,
and will of his contemporaries. Joined by Jules Lemaître, who
carried the attack to a popular audience, fed by the nationalism
of "l'Action Française," then at its height of prestige, and taken

1. Albert Schinz, *Etat présent des travaux sur J.-J. Rousseau* (Paris, 1941),
p. 5. For an update of this survey see Jacques Voisine, "Etat des Travaux sur J.-J.
Rousseau," *L'Information Littéraire* 16 (1964).
2. A statement made by Alphonse de Lamartine who, although a spiritual
child of Rousseau in his poetry, hated Rousseau's politics. Schinz, p. 22.

27

to an extreme by Ernest Seillière and Irving Babbitt, the offensive against Rousseau attributed to him responsibility for the French Revolution (not to mention Romanticism, at a time when that concept was at its lowest ebb of popularity). "Folly, savagery, ignorance, singularity, solitude, pride, and revolt, these are what the adventurer, nourished by the biblical marrow, erected on the altar in the name of virtue," Charles Maurras complained against Rousseau. "His own indignant and lamentive sensibility, dressed up as law, served him as decisive criterion against the universe" (Schinz, p. 77).

The phrasing of most of these attacks is similar: Rousseau is accused of violating something sacred, of substituting selfish or personal values for universal, normative ones, which is simply to say in general terms that he is making a transition from a classic to a romantic world view. For our purposes, however, the most significant statement of the charge is not made during the "grand offensive" of the years around the bicentenary, but arises out of the "Hume affair" during Rousseau's own period. Horace Walpole made explicit the herostratic analogy that is latent in the attacks of the succeeding generations, referring to Rousseau as *"the new Herostratus who burned the temple of Modesty in order that he be talked about."*[3] For his "crimes" against accepted standards of conduct and opinion Dr. Johnson declared Rousseau "to be one of the worst men to exist, a rascal who should be expulsed from society as in effect he was" (Schinz, p. 49).

In one sense the outrage of Rousseau's contemporaries that made them speak of him as though he were a monster is understandable. He had, after all, with the fire of his impassioned rhetoric, put a torch to the academic and Counter Reformation principles of art. It had been established in previous centuries that art could be used to glorify and propagandize for the state or the church, but not for the individual. Rousseau was no more a "Sun King" than Herostratus was an Alexander. Why, then, should either one expect to be immortalized? But Rousseau's "presumption" was a sign of the times: shortly after his death, seemingly at his instigation, the age of revolutions began bringing destruction in the name of the nobodies who wanted to be somebodies. In fact, as "the greatest single manifestation of envy as a social force

3. Voisine, *J.-J. Rousseau en Angleterre à l'Epoque Romantique: Les Ecrits Autobiographiques et la Legende* (Paris, 1956), p. 108.

in man's history," the French Revolution itself may be seen as herostratic (Schoeck, p. 167).

Rousseau's "legendary" association with the Revolution is significant for our theme, for he apparently knew, and tried to distinguish himself from, the herostratic types with which the salons abounded, all those "underprivileged" ones like himself who, in being allowed to mingle with their social "betters," developed a sense of injustice. The resultant passions fed the ambitions that led to the storming of the Bastille, the reign of terror, the invasion of Russia, and Waterloo. "Let us not mistake burning brains for sensitive hearts, as one does in society," Rousseau says, wanting to separate himself from this horde, "whose sole desire to shine animates their conversations, actions, writings. . . . Dedicated to their unique object, that is, celebrity, they do not heat up for anything in the world, take no real interest in anything. . . . Thus tranquil and cold-blooded regarding everything . . . they know only how to hate what is not themselves" (D, p. 205). Such is the self Unamuno knew only too well, as we shall see. But the flames that burned in Rousseau's heart are as herostratic as those consuming the brains of his fellows. Believing that "fate owed me something that she had never given me," ever conscious of his "internal worth," Rousseau indulged in a bittersweet feeling of injustice experienced as a "devouring but barren flame by which ever since my childhood I had felt my heart to be consumed in vain,"[4] the flame recalling, of course, the herostratic fire. The envy of which Rousseau felt himself the object throughout his later life, then, is, in part, the projection of his own shadow, of his envious desires for recognition.

At the same time, as he makes clear in the first *Discourse*, Rousseau, having identified herostratism (without using the term) as *the* modern feeling, opposes the struggle for distinction among men, especially among men of letters who, he says, suffer more from this vice than any other group. The strength of his opposition is itself a measure of his own suffering from this passion. Along with his general rejection of the accumulated inventions of progress in the arts and sciences, Rousseau singles out for blame the invention of printing—"the art of eternalising the extravagances of the human spirit"—for it is because of printing that "the danger-

4. *The Confessions of Jean-Jacques Rousseau*, trans. J. M. Cohen (Baltimore, 1954), p. 373.

ous 'reveries' of Hobbes and Spinoza will last forever" (CS, pp. 21–22). Dangerous perhaps, but Unamuno (apropos of his quotation out of context from *Emile*), basing his own expression of the "hunger for immortality" on Spinoza's definition of the essence of man as the effort to persevere in one's own being (ST, p. 38), is ready to cultivate extravagance itself as a method. Rousseau, on the other hand, closes his first *Discourse* with an admonition to all those without talent ("like himself") to be content with obscurity, to renounce the painful and unrewarding pursuit of a reputation, "without envying the glory of the celebrated men who immortalize themselves in the republic of letters" (CS, p. 24). In spite of his opposition to this syndrome, then, Rousseau never denies that it works—the men of letters *are* immortalized.

The "exemplary" quality for Unamuno in Rousseau's work is that as a modern, civilized man he bears witness to the same pain Unamuno feels. He diagnoses this envy, this pursuit of artificial immortality, as the illness of his age, which is what attracted Unamuno's attention in the first place, and, as an example for others, sets out to cure it in himself. The cure is of special interest since Rousseau is an illustration of Herostratus *after* the fire—of the problem involved not in acquiring fame but in living with it. All that survives of Herostratus is his legend, but Unamuno wants a *personal* immortality, wants to survive in human memory as *himself*. And he finds in Rousseau's struggle with the legend and the conspiracy a point of comparison.

With the advent of his writing career Rousseau deliberately tries to overcome Herostratus on his own ground with the intention, in works like the *Discourse on Inequality* and *Emile*, of guiding men away from envy, and later, in his confessional writings, to salvage from the envious his own reputation. At a point in *Emile* where he momentarily drops the mask of fiction, Rousseau describes his own "illness" along with the cure for it offered by the Savoyard Vicar: "The most difficult thing to destroy was a proud misanthropy, a certain bitterness against the rich and happy of the world, as if they were so at my expense, as though their supposed happiness had been usurped from mine" (E, p. 318). Here we have a classic definition, drawn, possibly, from St. Augustine's confession, in which envy is described as sorrow at another's prosperity and joy in his harm.

But of course their happiness has been usurped from you, Unamuno responds: "Los afortunados, los agraciados, los favoritos" are blameable for their well-being, declares Unamuno's Cain figure, Joaquin Monegro, representing what Unamuno thought of as Spain's chief vice. The sons of Abel, the "Abelites," invented hell for the "Cainites" to better enjoy their own good fortune: "Their enjoyment is in seeing, free of suffering, the suffering of others." No wonder, among people more capable of hating others than of loving themselves, whose success or happiness was dependent on the failure and misery of others, that both authors found their reputations under attack. The issue, then, was how to preserve one's identity in such conditions.

Considered in this light, the "Profession of Faith" included in *Emile* may be recognized as a more or less practical manual aimed at remedying or eliminating the psychological conditions later defined by Unamuno as "congoja" and "erostratismo." Indeed, a major function of Christianity has always been the containment of envy along with the other sinful passions. The Vicar states that a proven source of contentment in the world is to utilize oneself the attitude successfully manipulated by the "fortunate," that is, to appreciate one's own condition in contrast to the miserable of the world: "By avoiding always the vain appearance and showing me the real ills which it covers, he taught me," Rousseau says of his mentor, "to deplore the errors of my neighbors, to be moved by their misery, and to pity them rather than envy them" (E, p. 319). With the stratagem of pity Rousseau hit upon what Francis Bacon considered to be the only antidote to envy (Schoeck, p. 164). This adjustment of vision through an act of will is practiced throughout Emile's education; one never shows a child those people who are superior to him or better off than he is, but only those in a lower condition. Thus, "he enjoys at the same time the pity he has for the ills, and the good fortune which exempts him from them" (E, p. 270). To live happily in the civilized world, where the choice is to be either the envied or the envier, the mocked or the mocker, one must, in full awareness of the psychological realities controlling that world, devise envy-avoidance strategies.

Rousseau's strategy includes making the distinction between "amour-de-soi" and "amour-propre." "Amour-de-soi" is an absolute, instinctual sentiment that has reference only to the self and that was perverted into "amour-propre"—a viciously competitive selfishness—by the evolution or fall from nature into society. Self-love becomes an evil in the movement from an absolute to a relative frame of reference (E, p. 81). But, extended away from one's personal concerns to the general concerns of mankind, even "amour-propre" may become a virtue in that it provides one with the first experience of compassion or pity. Knowing at first only his own suffering, the child, aided by his imagination, experiences the desired expansion of self-love when he discovers the suffering of mankind in the tableau of the human condition: "All are born naked and poor, subject to the miseries of life, to the chagrins, the evils, the needs, the pains of every kind; finally, all are condemned to death. There you have what is truly man's lot; there is the thing from which no mortal is exempt" (E, p. 260). The universal death penalty eases the pangs of envy and schools the individual in the toleration of inequality in this life.

Unamuno makes a similar distinction between "egotismo" and "egoismo": "Spiritual love of oneself, the compassion one gains for oneself, could be called egotism, but is antithetical to vulgar egoism. Because from this love or compassion for yourself, from this intense desperation, because just as before birth you were not, neither will you be after death, you begin to pity, that is, to love all your neighbors and brothers in seemingness, miserable shadows who file from nothing to nothing, sparks of consciousness that glow a moment in the infinite and eternal darkness" (ST, p. 125). The only virtue of comparative living is that, properly manipulated, it may generate a pity that counteracts envy. On the other hand this solution has the disadvantage of forcing one to contemplate the certainty of one's *own* death along with that of the others.

Anxious to justify themselves against the charge of vulgar egoism, both authors, as we noted earlier, stress that their self-love is of the non-comparative, absolute sort, *not* dependent on the discomfort of others, that is, not herostratic—an attitude which leads them to imitate God rather than their fellow man. Their common problem is how to deal with the misunderstandings that arise from their self-direction; how, once they have attracted the attention of the crowd, they may preserve their "true" identity, as distinct from the legend created in the perceptions of others.

Living at a time when the self-other, intersubjective conflict was not the commonplace that it is today, Rousseau at first attributed the disparity between his self-concept and the opinions others held of him to the work of a conspiracy or plot originated by his closest friends—Melchior von Grimm, Denis Diderot, and the d'Holbach group. The motive, of course, was envy. They could tolerate his successful books, Rousseau thought, but their envy was aroused by his success as the composer of *Le Devin du Village* since music was not among their own talents.[5] But even more than his writing, it was his individualism, his "personal reform," his break with the customs of his times in order to bring his practice into conformity with his published preachings, that fixed their envy upon him (C, p. 429).

It is no doubt true that Rousseau was paranoiac, but his behavior with regard to the conspiracy is also that of a man obsessed with envy. His fear of "le regard," his sense of being constantly observed, "hemmed about by watchful and malevolent spies, distracted and anxious," resembles the fear of the "evil eye" cast by the envious neighbor that is the bane of many primitive and peasant cultures. His inability to accept gifts or favors, and his rage at and suspicion of the friends who attempted to help him demonstrate the axiom that the worst thing you can do for an envious man is a favor (Schoeck, p. 282).

There was nothing imaginary, however, about the "libelous" pamphlet "Le Sentiment des Citoyens," in which Voltaire attacked Rousseau, and which finally made Rousseau decide to act on his publisher's suggestion to write a memoir.[6] The "truth," he felt, would be his best defense against the legend. Ironically, the confession which he wrote to clear his name, because of its notorious "immodesty," only added fuel to the fires of envy.

"But since my name is fated to live, I must endeavor to transmit with it the memory of that unfortunate man who bore it, as he actually was, and not as his unjust enemies unremittingly endeavour to paint him" (C, p. 475: Cohen, p. 373). Here, in a sentence, is why Rousseau allowed himself to be drawn into the problem of the legend, to fall victim to the Herostratus factor. The fact that he dedicated the *Confessions*, the *Dialogues*, and much of the *Rêveries* to this theme of his legend and the conspiracy against

5. See F. C. Green, *J.-J. Rousseau: A Critical Study of his Life and Writings* (Cambridge, England, 1955), p. 53.
6. Jean Guéhenno, *Jean-Jacques Rousseau*, vol. 2, trans. John and Doreen Weightman (New York, 1967), p. 188.

it is a measure of how important it was to him. The disparity between his view of himself and his reputation in the minds of his
contemporaries is the primary motive for his shift from writing
about Man in the Enlightenment vein to writing as a "preroman-
tic" about self.[7] But just as his use of the written word to attack
those who built reputations with the word entangled him, at the
beginning of his career, in an embarrassing paradox, so now in the
conspiracy does Rousseau become entangled with the vice of
Herostratus—obsessed with his reputation, with the vain sound of
his name echoing through the ages, with the way others think of
him, a preoccupation that turned his original experience of writing
—an ecstasy of virtue—into the "source of all his misery."

In the beginning he made no attempt to be popular or to flatter
current fashions, but wrote as one who wished to live "beyond his
century." "Clashing head on with everything that is today the admiration of men," he declares in the preface to his first *Discourse,*
the one which launched his career, "I cannot expect anything but
universal condemnation . . ." (CS, p. 2). He is willing, in short,
to be notorious. Indeed, his attack on the arts and sciences bears
an allegorical resemblance to Herostratus's destruction of the
beautiful temple. But once the condemnation actually occurs,
his appeal to posterity reveals itself as a gamble. Having committed himself to "eternity," Rousseau feared that the conspirators
might be able to alter his identity after his death by falsifying his
writings (C, p. 670). Finally, however, there was no need for this
worry because, as he himself noted repeatedly in the *Dialogues,*
the alteration takes place in the reader's mind, not on the page.

There exist in time, then, two Rousseaus—the one in his own
books, known primarily to a few scholars, and the legend, the
symbolic Rousseau who exists in other people's books and in the
popular imagination. The opposition between the two could not
be more complete. The scholars are finding not the emotional
Rousseau of tradition, but a rationalist; not a proponent of a return to nature, but the prophet of a perfected civilization in the
future; not an opponent, but a friend of the arts and sciences; not

7. "La philosophie de Rousseau est donc avant tout doctrine de la conscience
et du rassemblement de soi, hostile par principe à tout inconscient. . . . Chacun
s'y pose à tout instant la question par excellence: 'Suis-je bien celui que je
pensais être' " (Burgelin, pp. 118-19). The authors' emphasis on the preservation
of their reputations is understandable since both assert that memory is the primary
integrative force of the personality (E, p. 344; ST, p. 13).

a Dionysian, but an Apollonian advocate of moral restraint; not
an anarchist but a statist, and so forth (Schinz, pp. 396-98). But
then the scholars are interested in the latent more than in the
manifest Rousseau. Meanwhile, the "living" Rousseau is the
legendary one, the romantic revolutionary, the Rousseau created
as much by the conspiracy as by himself, an example which was
not lost upon Unamuno.

At the same time, Rousseau has always had his defenders, including Unamuno. It is important to note that Unamuno came to
Rousseau's defense not to deny that the legendary Rousseau was
the real one, but to defend that legend. He agrees with Lasserre
and Lemaître that Rousseau is the origin of the sickness infecting
the modern age, but his interpretation of this view is radically
opposed to theirs. This point appears in the essay "El Rousseau
de Lemaître" and is a major clue to the tradition which binds Unamuno to Rousseau. Noting the "sadness" and "irritation" that he
felt upon reading the works of Rousseau's critics such as Lasserre
and Lemaître, Unamuno analyses with perfect accuracy the political and religious chauvinism underlying the charges of "monster" and "lunatic" directed by the French Catholics at the Swiss
Protestant Rousseau. Most important to our theme is the way in
which Unamuno universalizes the argument, embracing Rousseau
as the representative of a tradition of passionate, emotional men
under attack by Voltairean, cold, dry rationalists. He goes on to
discuss the anti-Rousseauists in terms of his own personal myth of
Don Quixote. The "supreme occupation" of these reasonable men,
in contrast to Don Quixote who was the butt of all jokes, is never
to be duped, never to be mocked or appear foolish. Thus the
"grand offensive" against Rousseau's reputation causes Unamuno
to associate him with the knights of madness—not only with Don
Quixote, but with Christ, mocked by Pilate and reviled by his
people.[8]

8. Having problems with his own persecutors, Unamuno, too, understands
Don Quixote's situation: "Porque hay una turba de locos que padecen de manía
persecutoria, la que se convierte en mania persequidora, y estos locos se ponen a
perseguir a Don Quijote cuando éste no se presta a perseguir a sus supuestos perse-
guidores. Pero, ¿qué es lo que habré hecho yo, Don Quijote mío para haber llegado
a ser así el imán de los locos que se creen perseguidos? . . . ¿por qué me cubren
de alabanzas si al fin han de cubrirme de injurias?" (CSH, p. 145).

In response to Lemaître's admission that in spite of writing so many "tonterías"
Rousseau broke much new ground for literature and for sentiment, Unamuno says,
apropos of the wise fool, "Y es natural. Leed entre los maravillosos ensayos de

This feeling of being ridiculous, of having been made a fool of, is in fact the herostratic emotion and is, as we shall see in the next chapter, the definitive experience of the identity crisis associated with the legend that causes one to become obsessed with fame.

It is ironic, finally, that Horace Walpole should relate Rousseau's "self-advertisements" to the legend of Herostratus, because Rousseau himself accused Grimm, the chief instigator of the conspiracy, of herostratism: "A time will come when one will have for the century in which Jean-Jacques lived," Rousseau says, speaking of himself in the *Dialogues*, "the same horror that this century holds for him, and when this plot immortalizing its author like Herostratus will pass for a work of genius and, even more, of maliciousness" (D, p. 296). Rousseau, then, recognizes the applicability of the Herostratus factor to his case, but only to say that not he, but his age, is the new Herostratus.

William James el titulado 'Los grandes hombres y su ambiente' y veréis cómo os explica que la absurda física de Aristóteles y su lógica inmortal fluye de la misma fuente." Meanwhile, Lemaître's common sense is simply dull and superficial. With Rousseau's victimization in mind Unamuno adds, "Y me acuerdo de nuestro Don Quijote, de aquel glorioso Caballero de la Fe, honrosísimo blanco de todas las burlas, ludibrio de las gentes todas y a quien un niño podía engañar; de aquel prodigo de valor que supo arrostrar, impávido, el ridículo. Cuando el temor de hacer el ridículo se apodera de un individuo o de un pueblo, están perdidos para toda acción heroica" (OCs, 3:1204).

3. The Tragicomic Sense of Life

At the present time, we must bring to light the subject, the guilty one, that monstrous and wretched bug which we are likely to become at any moment.
JEAN-PAUL SARTRE

The Rousseau who moves Unamuno, the one he places in the pantheon of mocked heroes in defiance of all the Voltaires of the world, is the paranoiac Rousseau, the Rousseau of the *Confessions* and the *Dialogues*, obsessed with the conspiracy of defamation. In fact, the specific sentiment of persecution which Rousseau felt in relation to the d'Holbach clique (which he held responsible for turning the citizenry against him) was generalized by Unamuno's day into a free-floating paranoia, an anguish rooted in the detranscendentalized condition of man who, to the degree that he is self-conscious, and hence aware of self-contradiction, feels ridiculous.[1] Although God is dead, the guilt and shame that, in a Christian world, could be identified with sin, do not disappear but persist as a profound embarrassment, a sense of foolishness, of absurdity. Let us review, then, Rousseau as the tragicomic fool relived by Unamuno in his readings.

Imposing not the dignity of tragic villainy but comic scorn, making of him not a Macbeth but a Caliban, the envious conspira-

1. Carlos Blanco-Aguinaga refers to Augusto Pérez as a "ridiculous man": "Unamuno's *Niebla*: Existence and the Game of Fiction," *MLN* 79 (1964): 190. The "ridiculous man" resembles the superfluous men of Russian fiction, including the characters of Turgenev, Dostoevski, and Chekov who feared that they were missing life and hence did not exist. Regarding the paranoia, see Emmanuel Mounier, *Introduction aux Existentialismes* (Paris, 1962), pp. 56–57. He notes that in Martin Heidegger and Karl Jaspers man is pictured as "investi, débordé, enveloppé de toutes parts par de l'être qui lui est opaque, ou hostile, qui le menace par sa proximité." Cf. Sartre's "visqueux"—"Comme dans l'univers du paranoïaque, tout est menace hors de moi, dirigée vers moi."

37

tors applied to him what Rousseau called "the favorite weapon of vice," that is, ridicule (CS, p. 142). "The gentlemen are less devoted to making of him an object of horror than an object of derision" (D, p. 126). The sense of being ridiculed was unbearable for Rousseau: "Among us, it is true, Socrates would not have drunk the hemlock, but he would have drunk in a much more bitter cup, insulting mockery and scorn, a hundred times worse than death" (CS, p. 11). The "holbachiens," Rousseau says, "work at nothing but to render me ridiculous," their whole purpose being to "defame me" (C, p. 429).

It was precisely this "mauvaise honte et la crainte des sifflets" which at first prevented Rousseau from carrying out his reform and breaking with the ways of his century. But finally, to preserve his identity against this conspiracy he chose to reveal himself as a fool. As painful as it was to tell, the truth was more to his credit than the lies of the detractors. The most extraordinary thing about the *Confessions* from Unamuno's point of view is that in recounting those things about himself that were most shameful and ridiculous Rousseau had to overcome something that he "feared more than death, more than crime, more than anything in the world" (C, p. 94). "It is not that which is criminal which costs the most to say, but that which is ridiculous and shameful" (C, p. 18). Nothing could arouse Unamuno's sympathy more than Rousseau's project to make a public spectacle of himself, to meet the ridicule of his contemporaries with a self-portrait that was more foolish, more trivial than anything his detractors might invent. By this sacrifice Rousseau demonstrates what Unamuno considers to be the only antidote to herostratic vanity.

The self that Rousseau most satirizes is the Quixotic Jean-Jacques who, mistaking life for a novel, went in search of "castles in Spain."[2] Of course the Quixotic Rousseau is precisely the one with whom Unamuno sympathizes, the Rousseau who, like old Quijano el Bueno, fell in love when the time to love had passed (C, p. 506) and so fell into the archetype of the "fool in love." In one of the most touching ironies of his life, although it is only one among his many "romantic follies," Rousseau discovered that his greatest desire—to experience true love (C, p. 492)—when

2. Critics who note the Quixotic element in Rousseau include Charles Hendel, *Jean-Jacques Rousseau: Moralist* (New York, 1934); Burgelin, p. 39: Voisine, "Self-Ridicule in *Les Confessions*," *YFS* 28 (1961–62):56, 58.

it finally was realized, brought upon him the thing he feared most, ridicule, ridicule not only in the eyes of others but in his own eyes as well. No wonder, then, that the very nature of experience seemed to be part of the plot to humiliate him. Thus, in his account of his unrequited passion for Mme d'Houdetôt, a girl so young that, as he says, he should have been her tutor rather than her suitor, Rousseau can only describe his condition with that self-excoriating term, "le ridicule" (C, p. 522).

Among the many deliriums, follies, and "comical catastrophes" he relates, involving everything from indecent exposure in his youth to his breakdown at the ceremony for reconversion to Protestantism in his maturity, one of the most revealing episodes is the affair with Mme de Larnage, which reflects and explains the pattern of the neurosis that finally engulfed him. Finding himself among strange traveling companions, one of whom is flirting with him, Rousseau begins his usual breakdown. The more he fears that he is being mocked, the more foolish he becomes. They all think he is quite mad when, for example, in reply to an inquiry as to how he slept, he says, like a buffoon out of the *commedia dell'arte*, that he does not know (having been asleep the whole time). Rousseau himself makes the *commedia* analogy, comparing himself to the marquis du Legs, a Pantaloon figure in a Marivaux play.[3]

To protect himself he seizes on the "clever" idea of passing himself off as an Englishman, although he speaks no English, just as in an earlier catastrophe he took employment as a musician although he knew no music. He repeatedly tries, in other words, to treat the world as a theatre where roles may be freely chosen, only to end up playing the fool. The important clue to his behavior in the Larnage incident, foreshadowing his later dealings with the conspiracy, is that, "by a perversity of which no one but I was capable," he "imagined them to be leagued together to make a fool of me" (Cohen, p. 238). Finally discovering Mme Larnage's sincerity, and the foolishness of his suspicions, Dudding (his alias) stops being the dud, and becomes instead lively, witty, and charming precisely because the company thinks of him as such, the conclusion being that he is whatever others see him as. To be himself

---

3. In France the *commedia dell'arte* was absorbed into legitimate drama through such authors as Molière and Marivaux: Martin Esslin, *Theatre of the Absurd* (New York, 1969), p. 287. Finding that his eccentricity has made him fashionable, Rousseau compares himself to "Polichinelle" (C, p. 435).

he must be alone. But in Unamuno's eyes, that Rousseau describes himself in mocking terms, immortalizing himself as a bad actor always out of character and exposed to the audience's derisive whistles, makes him one of the rare, exemplary heroes of the modern age in which the price of selfhood is not solitude but mockery.

All of the time and money Mme de Warens spent trying to train him to be a gentleman was wasted, Rousseau declares. She failed as a Pygmalion: he is the "my fair gentleman" who never was. In fact, Rousseau's sense of himself as a fool is as much the key to his character as it is to his relation with Unamuno.[4] So completely inept is he in social situations that, as he says, every attempt to conceal his ineptitude only exaggerates it. As a result, "though I am not a fool, I am very often taken for one. . . . I should enjoy society as much as anyone, if I were not certain to display myself not only at a disadvantage but in a character entirely foreign to me. The role I have chosen of writing and remaining in the background is precisely the one that suits me. If I had been present, people would not have known my value" (Cohen, pp. 115–16).

It is at this point that Unamuno feels Rousseau betrays his own brilliant defense to become a pessimist. Surrounded by the traps of the conspirators, Rousseau saw himself as "the object of their derision, the toy of their hate, *the dupe of their perfidious caresses*," and so decided that the best solution finally was to "flee to spare himself such painful sentiments" (D, p. 134). But Unamuno maintains that a retreat into solitude only intensifies the feeling of being ridiculous and, as Rousseau admits, amounts to a fear of being duped, a proud desire to not "hacer el primo" (SMB, p. 128). Unamuno, of course, has in mind the tradition of Saint John of the Cross. For a saint, one proof of humility is to accept public revilement. Unamuno's solution, for which Rousseau is himself a major precedent, is to take over as one's own the imposed condition. The essence of the comic sense—more accurately termed the tragicomic sense of life—is not only to know how to confront ridicule, but to actually "*make oneself ridiculous*" (ST, p. 274), which is not only the highest kind of heroism, but the only kind still possible. The ridiculous, as Fulgencio Entrambosmares advises, must be transformed into the sublime, a transfor-

4. See Alain Finkielkraut, "Bêtises de Rousseau," *Critique* 30 (1974): 955–72.

mation accomplished by willing the ridicule which entails "making oneself a spectacle so that the world is entertained" (SMB, pp. 128–29; ST, p. 274). In this fusion of pride and shame, vanity is refuted.

As a symbol of tragicomic man Unamuno points to Don Quixote, "a grave man . . . nor does one have any record that he ever laughed within although he made the entire world laugh" (DQ, pp. 172–73). Similarly, taking Molière's *Le Misanthrope* as an example of his special objection to comedies (which he held to be more of a moral threat than tragedies), Rousseau sympathizes with Alceste against the other characters, the audience, and the author, Alceste being the perfect image of "an upright, sincere, worthy man, a truly good man" (CS, p. 150), who is forced to bear ridicule from all sides. Rousseau's personal reading of the play that leads him to identify himself with the comic Alceste as a virtuous man exposed to ridicule is echoed later on a much larger scale in Unamuno's phenomenological self-identification with Don Quixote.

Rousseau agrees with Alceste's final words: "Je vais sortir d'un gouffre où triomphent les vices, / Et chercher sur la terre un endroit écarté / Où d'être homme d'honneur on ait la liberté." Unamuno, however, insists that the "true solitary" does not flee the crowd, but "is the one who begins to dance in the middle of humanity's market place and in full view of all his brothers, to the sound of the music of the celestial spheres, which he only, thanks to the solitude in which he lives, can hear" (EN 1:680). This kind of spectacle Unamuno calls "the most tragic ridicule, reflexive ridicule, that which one does before oneself, in the eyes of one's own soul" (ST, p. 280). *Internalizing* thus the battleground of Quixote—the confrontation with public mockery—Unamuno's solitary, far from losing his identity by making himself ridiculous, gains possession of it through the public recognition. With his self-ridicule in the *Confessions* Rousseau took the first necessary step beyond Don Quixote.

Although he has gone in turn one step beyond Rousseau, Unamuno fulfills the basic demand of Rousseau's anti-herostratic strategy, which is to abandon all relative, comparative living and to live only absolutely: Unamuno lives with others, but on his own terms. The hero, Unamuno emphasizes, is "he who takes his role seriously and possesses it and does not think of the gallery, nor does he care a straw about the public, but performs for real" ("al vivo") (AP, p. 52).[5] This attitude is similar to that of Rousseau, who, speaking of the fad for nature study, warns that "as soon as one mixes in a motive of self-interest or vanity . . . one no longer wants to know but to show that one knows, and in the forest one is simply on the world's stage, concerned with making oneself admired" (R, p. 99). Although there is a significant change of setting, the point is the same: it is the self-direction which counts, not whether one is in the forest or the city. Neither author is willing to accept an externally imposed identity.

Unamuno, then, recognizes Rousseau as a hero of reflexive ridicule, in spite of the latter's ultimate retreat from society. Unamuno gives Rousseau a central place as one of his "tragic" masters because Rousseau, a man of flesh and bone, not a Christ or a fiction like Don Quixote, shows Unamuno the way to live heroically even as a ridiculous man in an upside-down world. The principal difference between them rests on Rousseau's reluctance to be a dupe, for, as Jules de Gaultier and Pierre Lasserre both assert, one of the privileges of being French is never to be a dupe (ST, p. 285). "Sad privilege!" Unamuno responds as he embraces the "duped" condition Rousseau was forced to accept. A foreigner, after all, as the *Action Française* stressed, Rousseau did not manage to avoid being a dupe but played the fool publicly, for which Unamuno loved him with a deep sense of recognition.

Unamuno identifies himself, then, not with the solitary Rousseau, but with the Rousseau who found he could not step into the street without being surrounded by "objets dechirants" (R, p. 131), who describes himself in the *Dialogues* as being treated like the Governor Sancho Panza, greeted everywhere "with endless mocking bows" (D, p. 60), or, again a Spanish example, like Lazarillo de Tormes, carried from town to town displayed as a sea monster (D, p. 111). His feeling of being bound and gagged by the conspirators, considered in the light of his problems (as a champion of Italian music) with the French theatre, gave Rousseau further cause for empathy with the *commedia dell'arte* players.

---

5. Apolodoro illustrates that the herostratic wish may be literally as well as figuratively suicidal. Therefore, Unamuno urges, "Cúrate de la afección de preocuparte cómo aparezcas a los demás. Cuídate sólo de cómo aparezcas ante Dios" (DQ, p. 19). Rousseau agrees that only God can have a correct understanding of a man (D, p. 77).

His situation no doubt reminded him of the attempts by the *Comédie Française* and the French authorities earlier in the century to destroy the Italian troupe in France by forbidding all speech in their productions.[6]

Cut off from human communication, Rousseau gave himself up to the promenade and the reverie, wandering the streets and lanes in and around the city, becoming, wherever he went, an object of public curiosity. Pausing in his apologetics long enough to sketch a portrait of himself as public spectacle, Rousseau shows us Jean-Jacques in a state of complete distraction, exhausted by the delights of the reverie, staring blankly for hours at a poster that happened to depict the plan of attack on the Fort de Kehl, while a curious crowd gathered, arguing among themselves, after he had revived and gone on his way, what crime he could be plotting for which such a plan would be useful (D, p. 160). He expects us, it seems, to be reminded of that Greek spectacle, Socrates, so different from other men, who stood fixed in thought from one dawn to the next, we are told in the *Symposium*, surrounded by curious spectators.

Rousseau is here laughing at his mockers, such laughter being itself a "divine pleasure" according to Unamuno (SMB, p. 128). Contemplating the exhausting efforts of the conspirators on his behalf from the tranquil ease of the abyss which they worked so hard to prepare for him, Rousseau remarks: "Foresight working in vain, fear is even more active, yet the authors of such a project have without noticing sacrificed to their hate the repose of their remaining days. . . . And if Jean-Jacques loved vengeance he would have it guaranteed in the dread which, in spite of so many accumulated precautions, never ceases to agitate them" (D, p. 291). Unamuno's last laugh has exactly the same rationale. If someone has been planning and working for forty years to jump you, thinking all the while you have no means of defense, you can laugh at him, Unamuno says: "And in any case he will have been during those forty years the slave of his proposition, of his foolishness, and of foolishness in general, while you, the improvisor, will have lived" (N, p. 190). Thus do Rousseau's systematic

6. W. Smith, *The "Commedia dell'arte,"* (New York, 1912), pp. 220–21. Rousseau's identification of himself with Alceste further confirms his sense of living in an Italian farce: see Gustave Attinger, *L'Esprit de la "Commedia dell'arte" dans le Théâtre Français* (Paris, 1950), p. 157.

"laziness," his avoidance of foresight, and Unamuno's comic sense, his "a lo que salga" attitude, serve the authors against the conspiracy of envy.

To appreciate the continuity as well as the differences between Rousseau's and Unamuno's modes of handling the problem of the legend and the conspiracy, we must review those elements of the problem which are constant between the two cases along with those that have changed. The theme itself is consistent: will the Unamuno of the legend be the one he wants or the one the crowd imagines? Also unchanged is the nature of this crowd. The conditions that generated the conspiracy against Rousseau consisted of "a state of things where each one, pretending to work for the fortune or reputation of the others, seeks only to elevate himself above the others and at their expense" (OC, 2:968–69). Unamuno encounters the same hypocritical, hostile milieu: "Those who applaud you are whistling at you, who shout 'forward' want to prevent your march to the sepulchre [of Don Quixote]" (DQ, p. 19). He also understands the feeling of being victimized by a conspiracy, as is seen in Joaquin Monegro's complaint: "There is another solitude much more terrible . . . that of the one whom all despise, whom all ridicule. . . . That of one who cannot find anyone who will tell him the truth. . . ." (AS, p. 40). Joaquin's experience is similar to Rousseau's frustration over the "public secret" from which only he was excluded: in his presence everyone "pretended" to be normal, nor would anyone admit any hostility openly.

What has changed is that Unamuno is no longer able to believe in an essential, inner self. A contemplative contraction around a central core is not a possibility, for, like the tree that serves as a spiritual symbol for the narrator of *Don Sandalio*, the self is hollow. No wonder, then, that Unamuno chooses to expand his outer boundaries, the surface that is his only essence. No wonder, too, that he becomes obsessed with the subjectivity of others: "What am I now in your consciousness?" he muses with regard to his readers and nonreaders. "This [consciousness] is the mist, the 'nivola,' the legend, the life everlasting" (N, p. 62).[7]

---

7. Whereas Rousseau insisted that the others could not know his true self, but only he himself could (M, p. 38), Unamuno states that he himself cannot know his true self, but the others can. Rousseau's final reaction to the conspiracy is to renounce control over his external image: "If men want to see me other than

This one major change in the conception of human nature alters entirely the method Unamuno must use to "control" his self-image in the hostile subjectivity of the other.[8] A complete redefinition of "sincerity"—Rousseau's own special theme—is included in the change. In the absence of an inner self to which his role must correspond (a correspondence which Rousseau tried to realize through his personal "reform"), Unamuno turns to pure representation. That it is more important to *be* something—to be happy, for example—than to *appear* to be is a distinction that is lost for Unamuno. Already predominant in Rousseau's time when, as he says, "slaves and dupes of their self-love, men live not in order to live but to make others believe that they have lived," the age of Herostratus is now fully established.

The radical implications of the new conditions for sincerity may be seen in the turn Unamuno gives to Rousseau's definition: "And it is the obligation of sincerity that requires us to veil and conceal the entrails of our soul, because if we revealed them the others would see them as they are not, and thus we would lie" (EN, 1:817). The conspiratorial conditions—the public misunderstanding or subjective reading of a confession—are the same as those Rousseau faced, only the attitude of the confessor has changed. There will be no more apologetics for a misunderstood self, but a burlesque attack on the reader's certainty about the basis of his judgments in the first place.

In contrast with Rousseau's sentimental tone of self-love in the *Confessions* and his rationalism in the *Dialogues* (where he tries to reason through the conspiracy), the new confessional method is ironic and irrational. Acknowledging that in mocking a character like the philosopher Fulgencio he is mocking himself, Unamuno offers this self-accusation: "Not daring to express on his own account certain follies, he adopts the convenient device of putting them in the mouth of grotesque and absurd characters, uttering thus in jest what he perhaps seriously thinks" (AP, p. 9).

I am, what of it? Is the essence of my being in their gaze?" (D, p. 325). He concludes that he is the one he sees himself to be. But Unamuno gives up the idea of an essential self and accepts the "Unamuno of my legend, of my novel, he whom we, my friendly self and my enemy self and all the others, my friends and enemies, have made together" (OCs, 11:726; cf. CSH, p. 133).

8. For a definitive essay on the three stages of the search for the pure self after the breakdown of the medieval world view, see Gregor Sebba, "Time and the Modern Self: Descartes, Rousseau, Beckett," *Studium Generale* 24 (1971): 308-25.

The point is that the key to Unamuno's thought is not his herostratic "congoja"—the tragic sense—but his reaction to it with his
sense of the comic. "On what pretext must we hitch ourselves to
the ominous yoke of logic?" Unamuno demands. "Time, space, and
logic are the three greatest tyrants over the human spirit. Does
liberty signify, or could it signify, anything other than the eman-
cipation from logic, our saddest servitude?" (AP, p. 138). The
motive for this rebellion against logic, in other words, is the same
need for liberty as that Rousseau cites for his withdrawal from
men and time (M, p. 37). "Harassed" by a "vulgar atmosphere,"
"enwrapped by webs of cowardice" so that he has to "paddle in
the spatterings of slimy lies" (DQ, p. 13), Unamuno turns to the
defensive jest, the "burla." Because it is self-directed, the jest is
not ridiculous but sublime, that is, tragicomic. As we shall see in
the next chapter, this tragicomic sensibility provides for Unamuno
an escape similar to that which Rousseau discovers in the reverie.

To those who complain that his comic method amounts to the
desire to be "extravagant at all cost, to say strange things, and,
what is worse, to vent bile and evil humor" (AP, p. 9), Unamuno
ambiguously declares: "A writer's public has before and above
all the others the undisputed right to know when it is spoken to
in jest and when seriously, although it is true that it enjoys one
who speaks to it with a certain feigned seriousness or with a certain
feigned gaiety" (AP, p. 11). In the same passage, however, he also
attacks his own work as a "disrespectful" and "lamentable equiv-
ocation," an "obvious" prank. In short, never sure of the author's
sincerity, the reader eventually should stop trying to determine
the author's intention, Unamuno reasons. As a further trap for the
unwary, though, he goes through the pages underlining words at
random to give them a meaningless emphasis (N, p. 50).

Rousseau's attitude to accusations and criticisms from his
readers similar to those Unamuno received was less good-
humored and more openly defensive: he makes demands rather
than compromises. "And they are not permitted to ignore that,
when a man speaks seriously, one ought to think that he believes
what he says, at least to the degree that his actions or conversations do not gainsay him" (OC, 2:961). "They pretend that I do not
think one word of the truths that I have defended," he notes indig-
nantly, "and that in demonstrating a proposition, I never left off
believing the contrary; that is, that I have proved things so extrav-

agant, that one is able to affirm that I could not have defended them except as a game." If this be the case, he adds, how could his accusers maintain their belief in reason after he has used it with such success to demonstrate so-called "follies?" Unamuno takes his cue from this assertion and draws the irrationalist conclusion that Rousseau avoided.

Rousseau's rationalistic sincerity, from Unamuno's point of view, leads to an inability to cope with the ambiguous, multi-vocal character of experience. Rousseau suspected that there was a certain "madness" involved with his problem because "when I would say 'white' others make me say 'black' without my even knowing it" (D, p. 183). But he could not ascertain whether he or the rest of the world was crazy (C, pp. 683, 697).[9] He was so much confounded by the infinite potential for ambiguity in life and letters that, in order to counteract his "hermeneutic myopia," he began systematically to interpret events inversely (Finkielkraut, p. 965). Avoiding all opportunities for good deeds because he feared a trap that would force him to do evil (R, p. 81), Rousseau felt it necessary continually to read between the lines: too much up on the turns his acquaintances gave to meanings to be taken in, he maintained, regarding an associate's confidence, "I understood that beneath that air of politeness he thought to tell me an untruth" (R, p. 42). He feels justified in reading the surface as the opposite of what it appears since things have become so turned around that the world is "as far away from the virtues as it could be, to the point of losing the very notion [of the virtues] and mistaking their opposite vices for them" (D, p. 311). In an upside-down epoch, with all the notions of the good and the worthwhile "reversed," he finds himself living "à rebours" (R, p. 93). It is no wonder, given his inability to sort out surface from hidden meanings in a paradoxical world, that Rousseau longs for a reality in which "the exterior countenance [is] always the image of the heart's disposition" (CS, p. 4).

Having Rousseau's example as proof of the futility of such wishes, Unamuno decides to take the offensive by adopting an

9. Unamuno has the same problem: "It has occurred to me to fancy that either almost all others, especially in my Spain, are crazy, or that I am, and since all the others could not be, then I must be. And hearing the judgments they make on my sayings, my writings, and my acts, I think, 'Could it be that I pronounce other words than those I hear myself pronounce, or that people hear me pronounce other words than I pronounce?' " (CSH, p. 144).

ironic version of Rousseau's hermeneutic inversions, "a method that consists of inverting sentences" that enables him to turn concepts "inside out, like a stocking" (OCs, 11:751). He also, therefore, finds himself living "against the grain": "More than once I have been told that I usually see things of the spirit something in the way that we might see the material world if it were a cinematograph whose strip were running in reverse, going from the end to the beginning . . ." (EN, 1:814). Once the process begins, however, he discovers that there is no way to determine which direction is correct. It comes down to the same thing whether you say God created man or man created God (ST, p. 135).

This confused state does not trouble Unamuno, even though, like Rousseau, he claims that his religion is the search for truth (EN, 2:366), because he holds a theory of language which, like his theory of the personality, is the opposite of Rousseau's. Rousseau knew that absolute truth was impossible to communicate simply because language was incapable of representing a man's emotional reality: "The impression of the word is always weak," he says, defending the greater expressiveness of personal interaction through gesture and glance, "and one speaks to the heart by the eyes much more than by the ears" (E, p. 398). But for Unamuno truth is a worthy but inaccessible goal for a different reason: "The word was made to exaggerate all our sensations and impressions . . . perhaps to create them. The word and all manner of conventional expression, like the kiss and the embrace. . . . No one suffers or enjoys what one says and expresses, or what one believes that one enjoys and suffers; otherwise, one could not live. At base we are so tranquil" (N, p. 123).[10] In short, for Unamuno language both verbal and nonverbal is not fuller but emptier than it seems. With this attitude it is not surprising that he should recognize himself in Rousseau's description of those herostratic types, cold men with burning brains, who could heat up for nothing but their own celebrity.

The difference in attitudes to expression results, in part, from Unamuno's examination of his situation in the light of his predecessor's "mishandling" of the conspiracy. Take, for example, the "extravagant" behavior that attracted to Rousseau the attention

10. Sánchez Barbudo (p. 90) states that the Unamuno of conflict and doubt is the legend created by the author to cover the true self, "al de la calma, 'terrible calma' verdadera."

of the envious plotters in the first place. Undertaking in the *Dialogues* an extended apology for his actions and attitudes, Rousseau tries to convince his readers that his extravagance is not a deliberate, willed trick to capture the public eye, but simply the result of "doing what comes naturally." "The cause of the false judgments passed against J.-J. is that one always supposes that it costs him great effort to be different from other men, rather than that, constituted as he is, it would take immense efforts to be like them" (D, pp. 193–94). All of his actions, he maintains, in spite of their divergence from the normal pattern of conduct, are simply the result of following his temperament.

Since these efforts to explain himself did little to save Rousseau's reputation, Unamuno decides to try a different course. He theorizes that, in this paradoxical world, people ought to exaggerate their defects or peculiarities rather than mask them with apologies or simply take them as they find them, ought to convert their weaknesses into strengths, thus disguising in the only way possible their defect as such (OCs, 11:731). To give a physical illustration of his point Unamuno describes a hunchback with the attitude that "this is not a hump but a caprice I have of wearing a knapsack on my shoulders beneath my jacket." But the best application of the theory, Unamuno adds, is "in defects of an intellectual and moral order," and he goes on to declare: "And this, say what you like, is sincerity. Because there is nothing more sincere than pretending" (OCs, 11:738).[11] This role-playing is the jest on oneself and the world. But it is better to be "extravagant" than to drift pointlessly. Such is the advice that Fulgencio gives to Apolodoro, the modern Emile (AP, p. 79).

We realize how far from Rousseau Unamuno is here when we think of Rousseau's low opinion of the professional actor, for

11. Unamuno is working with the fundamental concept of Stoicism. The stoic's idea of how man fits into the world is best expressed in Epictetus's metaphor of world as theatre, the "central symbol throughout history of the search for authenticity." M. Berman, *The Politics of Authenticity* (New York, 1970), p. xxi. In this context, faced with "la burla," Augusto Pérez is advised by his old servant to practice the comic sense of life: "Confundir el sueño con la vela, la ficción con la realidad, lo verdadero con lo falso; confundirlo todo en una sola niebla. . . . El niño se ríe de la tragedia; el viejo llora en la comedia. Quisiste hacerla rana, te ha hecho rana; acéptalo, pues, y sé para ti mismo rana." Berman places Rousseau in the stoical tradition, as do Starobinski, *La Transparence et l'Obstacle* (Paris, 1957), p. 58, and Burgelin, pp. 302–4, at least as regards the world-as-theatre theme.

whom any sincere man would feel disrespect: "But a comedian on stage, displaying feelings other than his own: saying only what one makes him say, representing often a chimerical being, annihilates himself, so to speak, annuls himself with his hero; and during that oblivion of man, if anything remains, it is to be the spectator's toy" (CS, p. 187). The same fate befalls man, Rousseau believed, when he dons his social mask.

The provocative aspect of Unamuno's attitude, his sincerity, is that he does not disguise his role-playing, a stance which he believes to be an improvement on Rousseau's refusal to play any role. "I presume that some reader, upon reading this cynical and what could pass as immodest confession, this confession 'à la Jean-Jacques,' will turn against my doctrine of the divine comedy, or better of the divine tragedy, and become indignant, saying that I do nothing more than represent a role. . . . But what bothers this indignant reader is that I show him that he too is a comical person, novelistic and nothing less, a character whom I want to put in the middle of the dream of his life. Make of the dream, of his dream, life, and he will have saved himself" (CSH, pp. 170–71). Rousseau thought that to live in dreams he had to renounce life, but Unamuno does not acknowledge the discrepancy between dream and reality which Rousseau accepted. Rather, he blends the two realms so that it no longer matters whether you say existence precedes essence or essence precedes existence. Life is a dream —that is the tragic realization; but dreams can be life—that is the comic response.

Having considered here Unamuno's admiration for Rousseau as a hero of reflexive ridicule—the figure who dominates the *Confessions* and the *Dialogues*—we may turn now to another aspect of Rousseau—the figure in the *Rêveries*—which Unamuno cherishes but which he rejects as a model for his own project to live absolutely. In the next chapter we shall consider Rousseau's reverie, his attempt to live "here below" the life of the immortals, as a strategy of envy-avoidance.

4. Imitations of Immortality

*We need doctors and nurses who are
themselves sick; and now we understand the meaning of the ascetic
priest and grasp it with both hands.*
NIETZSCHE

That Rousseau finally chooses to be God's fool rather than
man's, that he attributes the conspiracy to God rather than to
men, is for Unamuno the ultimate mark of Rousseau's participation in the tragicomic sense of life. At the same time Unamuno
dislikes what seems to be Rousseau's betrayal of the tragic stimu-
lus, the irreconcilable conflict between the head and the heart,
which leads Unamuno to call Rousseau a pessimist who gives up
on the value of life by abandoning the struggle. And yet, true to
the archetype of the mystic, Rousseau does turn his "defeat" into a
kind of victory: "I can no longer avoid considering as one of those
secrets of heaven impenetrable to human reason the same work
which up to now I envisaged simply as a fruit of man's maliciousness. This idea, far from being cruel and heartrending, consoles
me, tranquilizes me, and helps me resign myself" (R, pp. 23–24).
Proclaiming that, as far as this world is concerned, all is finished
for him, that he is beyond reach of both harm and benefit from
others, Rousseau presents himself as "tranquil at the bottom of
the abyss, poor unfortunate mortal, but impassive *like God himself*" (R, p. 8, my italics). In other words, to abandon the herostratic struggle with fame is not to abandon the pursuit of immortality in this life. Rousseau's strategy is to redirect his envy away
from man toward God, to approximate immortality by imitating
God rather than by comparing himself to his image in other minds,
that is, to be a medieval fool rather than a Renaissance individ-

51

ual. The envy then dissipates because to thrive it requires a sense of equality. This plan is recommended in Plato's *Theaetetus*, which advises an escape from the world in order to imitate God as much as possible.[1]

Once again, in Rousseau's consoling abyss Unamuno recognizes his own feelings. His version of the crisis is as follows: "Neither does sentiment manage to make consolation a truth, nor does reason make of truth a consolation; but the latter, reason, proceeding on truth itself, on the concept itself of reality, manages to immerse itself in a profound skepticism and in this abyss rational skepticism meets with sentimental desperation, and from this encounter emerges a basis—a terrible basis!—of consolation" (ST, p. 97). The basis of consolation has changed from resignation to God's conspiracy to a "vital scepticism" created by "the clash between *reason* and *desire*," a clash from which is born "the holy, sweet, saving incertitude, our supreme consolation" (ST, p. 108). In contrast, Rousseau's consolation is based on certainty: "God is just," Rousseau declares, "he wants me to suffer, and he knows that I am innocent. There is the motive of my confidence, my heart and my reason cry out that it does not deceive me" (R, p. 24). Thus does Rousseau neutralize the frustrations of impotence that lead to *ressentiment*. As opposed to the pattern of destiny or fate that Rousseau sees in the events that brought him into conflict with his generation, providence is identified with chance by Unamuno (N, p. 190).

What bothers Unamuno most about Rousseau's solution is that the latter's tranquility is based upon the agreement of his heart and his reason. Prior to the conspiracy, the greatest threat to Rousseau's identity came in terms of certain contradictory moments in his life "where I became another and ceased to be myself" (C, p. 495). He found that in experience his good intentions translated into bad actions, actions which contradicted his true being: "Such is the lot of humanity; reason shows us the goal, and the passions separate us from it" (PN, p. 308). The only maxim of morality that is of any use in practice, therefore, is "to avoid situations that put our duties in opposition to our interests" (C, p. 60). The conflict between reason and feeling that virtue requires means that in society one must continually suppress one's feelings, be

1. J. A. Mazzeo, *Medieval Cultural Tradition in Dante's "Comedy"* (Ithaca, 1960), p. 13.

always doing the opposite of what one desires (D, pp. 165, 205). Such a condition is not only unbearable, but beyond the powers of Rousseau, who initiates instead his "personal reform," that is, his retreat from "this cruel morality" into nature. He makes an official request to be secluded in nature as in a prison, there to feed on dreams of freedom.

Finding himself rendered powerless by the conspiracy, Rousseau states: "Instead of surrendering to despair, I tranquilly give myself up to my laziness and to the care of Providence" (C, p. 334). Freed by his "systematic laziness," he achieves a negative image of virtue— he *avoids harming* anyone. Significantly, the renunciation of the combats of virtue is part of his imitation of God, for, as the Savoyard Vicar explains, "although we call God good, we do not call him virtuous, because he has no need of effort to do good" (E, p. 567). His isolation and attempted independence from his fellow men is a further application of the imitation: "A truly happy being is a solitary being; God alone enjoys an absolute happiness" (E, p. 259). Thus, when he says, "I resolve to no longer attach myself to anyone, but to remain independent by turning my talents to account . . ." (C, p. 387), he indicates his intention to approximate as closely as possible the happiness of God.

Rousseau meets the threat of disintegrative combat between reason and feeling—the tragic sense of life—by addressing himself to the problem of desire. "It is the disproportion of our desires and our powers that causes our misery. A sensitive being whose powers equalled his desires would be an absolutely happy being" (E, p. 63). In imitation of this happiness, Rousseau sets out to balance his desires with his powers. "The real world has its limits, the imaginary world is infinite; not being able to enlarge the one, let us contract the other" (E, p. 64).[2] Since to be divine is to be self-sufficient, anything that shows one's dependence or insufficiency is a sign of weakness—a weak being is one whose needs are greater than his strengths. Any attempt to realize one's desires is an admission of impotence. In Saint-Preux's words, "he who wanted to build a high tower did well to want to carry it all the way to the sky; otherwise he would have raised it in vain, the point

2. The decision that initiated the personal reform was itself creative of harmony between the head and the heart. He could have no confidence in the principles he fixed to live by unless his heart sustained his reason (R, p. 37).

at which he would have stopped serving but to reveal from a greater distance the proof of his impotence" (NH, p. 532). The proper strategy, rather, is to contract one's being to the inner center of the self "like an insect at the middle of its web" (E, pp. 65, 68).

Rousseau bids adieu to his century with the intention of living totally at peace, "in an eternal leisure." Such is the life of the "blessed in the other world, and from now on I will make it my supreme happiness in this one" (C, p. 761). With his attitude of divine objectivity that permits him to look with indifference on all the trials of life, including the prospect of his own death that troubled him during the conflict with the "holbachiens," Rousseau discovers an escape from the anguish of herostratism, from the need for fame. During the conspiracy the inner reality of others came to constitute hell for Rousseau: "What is the need to go look for hell in the after life? It is present in this one in the heart of the wicked" (E, p. 345). Unamuno, of course, considers the other's heart a heaven to be invaded. But now Rousseau is able to say that the interior dispositions of his contemporaries "cease to be anything for me; I see them now as nothing more than masses differently moved, deprived from my point of view of all morality" (R, p. 110).

The primary models for Rousseau's simulation of divinity are the child and the savage, the two creatures closest to living according to his conception of God. His laziness, thus, is not that of social man, but of the child "who is ceaselessly in motion without doing anything" (C, p. 762). Those aspects of his system not satisfied by the child model are fulfilled by the savage: "Wandering in the forests, without industry, without words, without a home, without war and without connections, without any need of his fellow men or any desire to harm them, perhaps even without ever recognizing any one of them individually," the savage, Rousseau says, is "subject to few passions, and is sufficient unto himself" (CS, p. 63). The two models coalesce, because in the primitive state "man perpetually remains a child." The traits represented by these models are those Rousseau identifies as being of the original self prior to the overlays of society and, in their similarity to his idea of divinity, make his imitation of God, he believes, viable.[3]

3. Burgelin notes Rousseau's "metaphysics of laziness," p. 131, as well as his temptation to be God, p. 425. Cf. I. Benrubi, "L'Idéal Moral chez Rousseau, Mme

Once the break with society is made, Rousseau discovers in his imagination the key to his character and the solution to the tension between desire and power. Whatever the object of his desire may be, he is able with the imagination to transcend all obstacles and frustrations separating him from it so that "his fictions become dearer to him than the realities themselves." In the reverie, "to desire and to enjoy are for him one and the same thing" (D, pp. 199–200). The conflict between the head and the heart is resolved, then, by locating the sphere of happiness entirely within. Far from having to reduce his desires down to nothing as would be necessary in society, Rousseau finds in exile and solitude a way to make desire and fulfillment simultaneous. This experience of the reverie, by providing access to the pure feeling of existence, of perfect self-presence, is the ultimate phase of absolute living. As long as this state lasts, "one is self-sufficient like God" (R, p. 71). Thus does Rousseau experience in this life the immortality that he thinks is the only kind worth having—an absolute existence purified of the herostratic taint, free of all opinion—even though it is as illusory as the herostratic immortality of fame.

Alone on his island, drifting in a small boat on a lake, or lying beside a quietly flowing river, Rousseau manages to experience in the reverie a pure state of being that also appealed very much to Unamuno.[4] The experience, after all, particularly as recorded in the fifth book of the *Rêveries*, is the one pointed out by the existential critics as the paradigmatic encounter with the cogito itself. In a discussion of Isaac Walton, Unamuno shows that he has encountered the contemplative, escapist powers of the water-induced reverie in exactly Rousseau's terms: "Stretched out next to a river, letting oneself be lulled to sleep by the water, one arrives at something that is like relishing life itself, naked life. . . . While the lulled intellect rests we feel the abounding concert of our organism's energies, and that is when one perceives something of what we could call the music of the body. . . . Liberated from the obsession of life, we enjoy it as its possessors, without suffering it like its slaves" (OC, 3:518–19). No aspect of the reverie

de Staël et Amiel," *Annales* 27 (1938):42: since man's nature is derived from God, to exist according to one's nature is to imitate God. Cf. Starobinski, *L'OEil Vivant* (Paris, 1961), p. 147: Rousseau's imitation of the child and of God are opposite extremes of nullity and infinity, yet come from the same source.

4. See the excellent study by Carlos Blanco-Aguinaga, *El Unamuno Contemplativo* (El Colegio de México, 1959).

is left unexplored or unappreciated by Unamuno, as this celebration of its delights indicates: "Oh, who might prolong this sweet moment and sleep in it and in it eternalize himself! . . . Insatiable desire sleeps and does not even dream; habit, saintly habit reins in my eternity; the disillusionments have died with the memories, and the hopes with the fears!" (ST, p. 46). Everything Rousseau described is here—the solitary man seated near the water in a state of perfect peace, suspended outside past or future, with the rhythmic repetitions of an unreflective, habitual life replacing the need to think, will, or desire (R, p. 70).

To relate the eternal to the temporal Unamuno develops the concept of "intrahistory," which is almost identical to the approach to life Rousseau describes, particularly the life-style practiced in imitation of primitive man. "He gets up, goes to bed, eats, works, leaves and returns at the same times without willing it or knowing it," Rousseau says, describing the life he led in imitation of the savage. "All the days are cast in the same mold; it is the same day always repeated" (D, p. 189). Unamuno's Pedro Antonio, Ignacio's father in *Paz en la Guerra*, recalling Unamuno's praise of habit, exemplifies this quotidian level, the "monotony" of the common man's life in which one enjoys "the novelty of each moment, the delight of doing the same things every day, and the plenitude of his limitation" (PG, p. 13). Pedro lives, as Rousseau tried to live, "in the reality of himself and not in the appearance of the others." His existence, Unamuno adds, "flowed like a gentle river." Living on this level, Rousseau is able to ignore "the instability of the things of this world of which the water's surface offers me the image" (R, p. 68). Unamuno, too, characterizes the passing show of life as "the surface of the sea" (ETC, p. 27) while intrahistory is the depth. The appeal of a work like the *Confessions* to Unamuno, who believes that the significant element of life is not the events of recorded history but the "alluvion of the insignificant" (DQ, pp. 165–66), is that it is itself an "intrahistory," based on the idea that "it is in the trifles that the natural reveals itself" (E, p. 287).

As much as he is tempted by Rousseau's "system," and while he continues to value the contemplative experience, as Blanco Aguinaga has demonstrated, Unamuno cannot confine himself to it. Properly understood, such serene contemplation, he says, provides a transcendental resignation which should be "the mother of

temporal unresignedness, to never be content here below . . ."
(PG, p. 249). Removing himself from the community, Rousseau
abandoned the gadfly role which Unamuno takes to be the philosopher's chief duty: "It is necessary to agitate the masses and
shock and winnow men and launch them against one another, in
order to see if in this way they break their crusts in the mutual col-
lision, and pour out their spirits, and mix, mingle, and confuse
one with the other and coagulate and forge once and for all the
true collective spirit, the soul of Humanity" (OCs, 3:608). Although with his ideal of "transparency" Rousseau wished that all
men would drop their masks and disguises to reveal their true
being to one another, he did not, from Unamuno's point of view,
do enough to *make* it happen.

The difference between the two men regarding the theme of reverie, then, comes down to their respective attitudes toward resignation, or pessimism. There is an ever present temptation in Unamuno's world, exemplified by Pachico's "deep resignation" (PG,
p. 248), to follow Rousseau's renunciation of society and to with-
draw into the absolute self of the imagination. Rousseau wanted
self-consciousness without suffering the pain of self-contradiction.

Unamuno, on the other hand, views Rousseau's isolated self-
focus as too similar to unconsciousness itself, and so explicitly
reverses the tendency displayed in his own earlier Rousseauistic
writings: "I know that I myself on other occasions and in other
writings have sustained and affirmed that liberty is consciousness
of necessity, consciousness of the law, that man ought to try to
want whatever happens so that thus things happen that he wants,
but these are no more than efforts with which I want to delude myself and reflections that I make in order to enclose the infinity
of space in the stunted cage in which I am condemned to live . . ."
(AP, p. 138). He cannot live in the peace of his dreams, cannot si-
lence the objections of reason. Not that Rousseau, too, did not
confront this conflict when he adopted the principles of his reform:
". . . who will protect me from despair if in the horror of my fate I
no longer see anything but idle fancies in the consolations furnished by my reason? . . . I find in them insurmountable difficul-
ties which are impossible for me to resolve and yet which do not
prevent me from persisting" (R, p. 36).[5]

5. In this moment of self-doubt, remarking that his generation finds truth and

Rousseau's choice of solitude, in Unamuno's opinion, approximates only "a false immortality, one in name only" (ST, p. 53). Although he suffers as much from what he calls "Flaubert's diease"—a hatred and fear of the mass of men—as Rousseau does, Unamuno considers society indispensable to the "deepest morality" of "mutual imposition": "to make efforts to stamp others with our stamp, to perpetuate ourselves in them and in their children, dominating them, in order to leave our imperishable mark on everything" (ST, p. 243). Immortality, now, cannot escape Herostratus completely.

Unamuno, then, finds in Rousseau's response to the conspiracy two fundamental things that mark the similarity of their problem: first, that the only way to satisfy one's hunger for immortality is to make of one's life a ritual imitation of God; second, that the key to this imitation is the relation between desire and the power of fulfillment. On the latter point, however, Unamuno's strategy is the opposite of Rousseau's because, for one thing, they are working with different conceptions of God. Unlike the tranquil, impassive God pictured by Rousseau (similar to Unamuno's description of the rationalist's God), Unamuno's God Himself participates in a Christ-like suffering. He is limited by the matter of the universe and, like man, is a consciousness suffering in a struggle to be free of all unconsciousness, of all inert matter. To believe that man is made in God's image (and vice versa) means that "just as I suffer to be Him, so does He suffer to be me and each one of us" (ST, p. 185).

To imitate God, then, requires suffering. And the greatest source of man's suffering, Unamuno says, is "to aspire greatly and achieve nothing. . . . We can undertake anything or almost anything with our understanding and desire, nothing or almost nothing with our will. Nor is contemplation happiness, no! if this contemplation signifies impotence" (ST, p. 127). Therefore every tactic Rousseau developed to protect his contemplative retreat and disguise his impotence Unamuno now reverses. He insists that the truly saving faith consists not in harmony, but "in maintaining this battle between the heart and the head, between sentiment

---

evidence in a system contrary to his own, Rousseau says: "Je me crois sage, et je ne suis que dupe, victime et martyr d'une vaine erreur" (R, p. 37); the editor marks this passage as evidence of the difficulty Rousseau had in conciliating his heart with his reason.

and intellect . . ." (DQ, pp. 124–25). Instead of Rousseau's great maxim of morality to avoid conflict, Unamuno advocates a "moral de batalla." In the struggle against obstacles one attains self-consciousness, a full sense of one's own being: "Pain is the road to consciousness, and it is through it that living beings come to have consciousness of themselves" (ST, p. 127). And the greater the capacity for suffering one has, the closer to divinity one comes since God is universal consciousness (ST, pp. 183–84). But one must never merge with God as Rousseau seemed to want to merge during his mystical identifications with nature. Rather, eternal life should be a Purgatory, a consciousness not only of seeing God, but of seeing oneself doing so, distinct and separate, at the same time (ST, p. 204).

Unamuno's answer to the disparity in man between desire and power is to take the offensive—to expand the individual self until it *is* everything (and everyone) else, to try for the all—whereas Rousseau takes a defensive stance, attempts nothing, and tries only to protect the self from invasion by others. "The evident impossibility of obtaining them [his desires] detaches them," Rousseau says; "wishes without hope do not torment" (E, p. 568; cf. D, p. 15). Unamuno, on the other hand, declares that "our excellence consists in expanding ceaselessly toward the inaccessible" (OCs, 4:30). The need to preserve his individuality led Rousseau to contract his being, in contrast to the average practice he noted among his fellows where "each one extends himself, so to speak, over the entire earth, and becomes sensitive over all this great surface. Is it surprising that our ills multiply at all the points where we can be hurt?" (E, p. 67).[6] Strange that we fear death so much, he adds, since the part of the world that dies—ourselves—we ignore while alive and give all our attention to that part which remains—the outer world.[7]

Rather than fight against this tendency of man to live elsewhere, for others, Unamuno chooses to exploit and exaggerate it. The way contemporary man fulfills the need for divinity is to absorb the universe into himself: ". . . to extend his boundaries to infinity, but without breaking them. He does not desire to break

6. The theme of expansion-contraction is central to both authors. Rousseau's attitude is that "l'homme en société cherche à s'éteindre, l'homme isolé se resserre. . . ." *Essai sur l'Origine des Langues,* ed. C. Porset (Bordeaux, 1970), p. 97. His other dichotomy is that the youth expands, the old man contracts.

7. Unamuno refers to this phenomenon as "topofobia" (ST, p. 283).

down his walls and leave everything in unobstructed, communal, undefended land, confusing himself and losing his individuality, but desires to carry his walls to the extremity of creation and to embrace everything within them. . . . He aspires to be the Universe, to be God" (ST, p. 185).[8] Man is man "only when he wants to be more than man," Unamuno states (DQ, p. 39). Drawing on the lesson of the fortunate fall, in which Adam, by wanting "to be like a god," learned to find strength in his weakness and glory in his degradation—key to the abyssful life—Unamuno defines the modern hero as one who is not satisfied with just being who he is, but is who he *wants* to be. In all of his discussion, including his example that Lucifer's fall was due to proud complacency and self-satisfaction, Unamuno directly contradicts Rousseau's belief that "the rebel angel who failed to recognize his nature was weaker than the happy mortal who lives in peace according to his. Man is very strong when he is content to be what he is; he is very weak when he wants to raise himself above humanity" (E, p. 65).

In fact, Rousseau sacrificed the self he wanted to be, the self of virtue and goodness which, he says, he could not attain but could only admire while painting its "divine simulacrum" in his imagination (D, p. 167). He tried for six years to become the virtuous man, the socially adept moralist who could crush the sarcasms of his enemies the way one might crush an insect between one's fingers, as he says. But after he had lived thus in what he described as "the one state in the world most contrary to my nature," the second "revolution" of his personality, prompted by the conspiracy of envy which rose up to challenge his virtue, began, "and restored me to nature, above which I wanted to raise myself" (C, p. 495). The difference between the authors here is *not* that Rousseau denies the power of suffering to create a sense of selfhood, but that Rousseau finally cannot support that suffering and so must seek an alternative means to the experience of his own existence. Like Unamuno, who appreciated the reverie but rejected it as a method, Rousseau, it must be said, also tried Unamuno's way of virtuous suffering. He recognized that suffering

8. "Este problema de la existencia de Dios, problema racionalmente insoluble, no es en el fondo sino el problema de la conciencia, de la ex-sistencia . . ." (ST, p. 163).

characterizes the human condition, granted that it benefits man
to the degree that it makes him self-conscious, insisted that suffering is preferable to feeling nothing at all, but finally states:
"There are kinds of adversity that elevate and reinforce the soul,
but there are also those which demolish and kill it; such are the
ones of which I am the prey" (R, p. 82).

Rousseau's strategy for the fulfillment of his existence was to
deal with his metaphysical desire, his existential envy, by means
of a systematic laziness involving the daydream as method, a
strategy the success of which required the sacrifice of his reputation, buying present peace at the price of alienation from his
legend. But Unamuno wants to cure himself of the ontological
illness—the "furious hunger for being, the appetite for divinity"—
without making Rousseau's sacrifice (ST, p. 14). He feels that he
can have it both ways by maintaining Rousseau's strategy—the
imitation of immortality—while replacing Rousseau's specific
method—the daydream—with the jest.

The purpose of the tragic farce as a method, of course, is to
counter the ridicule used by social man to eliminate the hero,
the man who *will* be an individual. Embodying, along with his
pupils and disciples, the comic method (the attack against logic
through the creation of self-parodies), the philosopher Fulgencio
embodies the method and all of its interconnections with Unamuno's primary concerns. Art originated, he says, *in the thirst for
immortality*, or, more specifically, in "el juego." "The game is an
effort to depart from logic, because logic leads to death" (AP, p.
111). The incorporation of play into his method of creation is a
chief way in which Unamuno's comic sense is an imitation of God:
"That is the mystic agony—it proceeds by antithesis, paradoxes,
and even tragic playing on words. Because the mystic agony plays
with words, plays with the Word, with Being. . . . As perhaps God
played in creating the world" (AC, p. 27). The use of language
is very important to the imitation, for "the metaphor, the parable,
and the paradox are divine language in man's mouth." Unamuno
tells us explicitly that the practice of the comic method is an imitation of God using as an example, significantly for the relation
to Rousseau, the language state of a child: "He trained himself
in the only divine faculty," Unamuno says, narrating the story of
the "wonder child," Apolodoro, "mocking logic. He awakened

the holy sense of the comical, delighting in every incongruency and every absurdity" (AP, p. 58).

Instead of Rousseau's righteous attack in the name of virtue against progress in the arts and sciences, Unamuno now mocks this progress with almost an element of Dadaism:[9] "If there have been those who have mocked God, why can't we mock Reason, Science, and even Truth? And if they have snatched away our most intimate, essential hope, why shouldn't we confuse everything in order to kill time and eternity and in order to revenge ourselves?" (N, pp. 52–53). The "burla" thus functions as the basic device of the tragicomedy, since, according to his own definition, to kill time is the essence of the comic, and to kill eternity is the essence of the tragic (SMB, p. 16). The jest circumvents the tragedy just as Rousseau's dreams circumvented the obstacles to the fulfillment of his desires.[10]

The comic sense, it must be stressed, requires a balance between being the mocker and being the mocked (AP, pp. 141–42). The "burladores" die comically, he explains, while for the "burlados" there is tragedy, "the noble part." But with his antithetical, tragicomic world view, the ridiculous man is neither victim nor assailant but "héautontimoroumenos"[11]—he is his own worst mocker because he knows he cannot know himself and so must suffer comic self-contradiction.[12]

Referring to his writing as self-surgery, Unamuno makes explicit the metaphysically compensatory function of his books (ST, p. 96). The ugly, herostratic drive to incorporate all other personalities that originates with the tragic sense is transformed finally by the comic sense into a martyrdom, a sacrifice of pride

9. Cf. W. Haftmann, *Painting in the Twentieth Century*, vol. 1 (New York, 1967), p. 182: "There Hugo Ball, a German philosopher and writer . . . had launched the Cabaret Voltaire, which he conceived as an instrument for the reassessment of moral, cultural, and social values. The method: buffoonery."

10. See Frances W. Weber, "Unamuno's *Niebla*: From Novel to Dream," *PMLA* 88 (1973):209–18. A major article on evasion in Unamuno—his preference for dream over reality. The gadfly status is a mask: Unamuno, as much as Rousseau, chose to hide himself and write, except that his distance is intellectual, ironic, rather than physical, as in Rousseau's flight to nature.

11. According to Georges May, Rousseau's contradictory nature makes him the prototype of "l'héautontimoroumenos." *Rousseau par lui-même* (Paris, 1961), p. 42.

12. ". . . et j'y vins bien confirmé dans l'opinion déjà prise que le Connais-toi toi-même du Temple de Delphes n'était pas une maxime si facile à suivre que je l'avais cru dans mes *Confessions*" (R, p. 42).

through which one at least deserves immortality and even gets a taste of it by imitating God rather than by negatively comparing oneself to one's neighbor and achieving selfhood at his expense.

By mocking himself Unamuno conforms to a world in which even God, if there is one, is part of the conspiracy against the individual. History, Unamuno suggests, might be nothing but "God's laughter," with each catastrophe nothing but "guffaws that resound like thunder while the divine eyes run with tears of laughter" (CSH, p. 173). Thus to laugh at tragedy (an impossibility according to some aestheticians) is to imitate God. Rousseau too, having assigned to God the responsibility for the conspiracy, entertains momentarily the Cartesian hypothesis of God as Evil Deceiver, equivalent to the malicious enchanter who plagued Don Quixote, a God who reneges on his promise of eternal life. "Tu m'as trompé!" Rousseau wails bitterly, once again the dupe. Reasoning, however, with buffoon's logic that the very injustice of this world proves the necessity of a just afterlife, Rousseau feels reassured for, after all, God's "raison d'être" is to guarantee immortality (E, p. 343; Schinz, p. 496). Unamuno loves a dupe who reasons so sublimely.[13]

If God himself wants to make fools of us then we must look for the source of Being in foolishness. And the laughter provoked by the breakdown of logic is nothing other "than the corporal expression of the pleasure we feel upon seeing ourselves free, even for a brief moment, from this ferocious tyranny . . ." (AP, p. 139). Each one of us plays a role which seems to be determined, Unamuno says, drawing upon the ancient analogy, but the actor may add a bit to the role and in this momentary escape from determinism, in this moment of divine freedom, this metadramatic moment called "la morcilla," lies the pure experience of our existence, our self-presence, which is exactly what Rousseau sought in the reverie. Unamuno takes seriously the literary phenomenon of the character's independence from the author, speculating that man too may escape from his creator's intentions; this role as

13. Rousseau's personal reform is the systematic application of a negative principle similar to the free will exercised by Descartes, who asserted his existence in the face of a potentially evil deity by refusing to act. Like Sartre after him, Rousseau discovers the ultimate source of man's freedom, and hence of his identity, in the power to say no: "I never believed that man's liberty consisted in doing what he wants, but in never doing what he does not want" (R, p. 86).

artist—the maker of creatures who have being apart from the author's being, who have free will—is his ultimate imitation of God. In the words of one of his own rebellious entities, "It is necessary to cultivate the comic sentiment of life, no matter what that Unamuno says" (SMB, p. 125).[14]

The comic sense and the "burla," finally, serve the purpose in Unamuno's work that laziness and the reverie serve in Rousseau's, the purpose being through the imitation of immortality to cope with the herostratic madness discovered in society. Unamuno's method is the active, aggressive equivalent of Rousseau's passive, defensive one that, with his inner void, Unamuno tried and found wanting. Ultimately both men see life as a kind of dream, preferably a waking dream, with the true reality of life being determined by the subjective consciousness of the individual. After developing extensive theories of their respective strategies—the daydream and the farce—both admit that their conduct is an evasion, an illusion of freedom in defiance of the concrete, phenomenal conditions in which they find themselves. Although Rousseau is much quicker than Unamuno to admit the illusory, negative quality of his chosen reality, Unamuno sometimes acknowledges that his notion of escape from logic is an illusion fostered during moments of "vagoroso ensueño," that is, during flights of reverie (EN, 1:814). Unamuno's case is complex because he does not flee the community, but remains in it using his gadfly, engaged status itself as a distraction from his potential despair. In any case, the evasions of both men are transcendentalist efforts to circumvent the petty, conspiratorial world of envious, mocking, or traitorous others, as well as to suppress these same qualities in themselves, and to attain the state of absolute, autonomous selfhood. Although both authors set out to imitate God, they have different conceptions of God—a self-sufficient, tranquil, impassive, happy God contrasted with a suffering, conscious, sadistic God—which accounts for the differences in their strategies.

Rousseau distinguishes between the actual and the dream worlds, plays his identity-fulfilling role as primitive and child

14. Unamuno's confrontation with his characters, a device later made famous by Pirandello, is a version of the Pygmalion theme so important to Rousseau. Pierre-Maurice Masson refers to "le pygmalionisme" in Rousseau, defined as "cet état d'esprit où l'illusion devient d'elle-même la réalité" (see Burgelin, p. 178). Berman also discusses the "Pirandellian interludes" in Rousseau, pp. 294–97.

in the former and confines his fantasies to the latter, while Unamuno fuses the two realms, saying that the actual, everyday life is based as much on pretending and illusion as are dreams themselves. In both cases the essence that we are is achieved and experienced, if only momentarily, in the dream-role of fantasy of the reverie or in "la morcilla" that we add to our life-role by exaggeration. The similarities extend to the structure and techniques of the methods, in that the comic sense as much as the reverie involves a "laisser-aller" or "a lo que salga" nonsystematic mode of thought. The modes include a similar "exaggeration" of a natural or temperamental inclination or weakness—Rousseau's "laziness" and Unamuno's capriciousness—which turns a defect into a virtue. In short, Rousseau's applied laziness, that has as its irrational center the dream, and Unamuno's comic sense, based on the mockery of logic, are both developed as the authors' definitive cures for the illness of the age, for metaphysical desire.

It is a misrepresentation, then, to say that, having lost his faith in God, Unamuno simply became a Herostratus. Both authors react to the discovery within themselves of herostratic envy, the obsession with the subjectivity of others, in a way that turns herostratic nihilism into an affirmation. Unamuno sums up this response in the concluding appendix of *Niebla*: "And this is how all those fools ought to affirm themselves," Augusto Pérez says. "Instead of trying to oppress another's personality they ought to exert themselves in exalting their own to the point of bursting" (N, p. 190). For Unamuno, Rousseau is *the* exemplum of this message.[15]

Keeping in mind what was said in the first chapter regarding Unamuno's theory of literary reincarnations, that the discovery of his own thoughts in the works of other men could be a proof of immortality, we may now be able to appreciate why, and in what way, Unamuno might respond to Rousseau, might find himself living again as a Rousseau, speaking to him within himself as the perfect comrade Rousseau missed in life. You believe you are alone, so alone that you are not even with yourself, Unamuno says, which is the price of non-comparative living, but all the

15. Rousseau points out that the man who lives alone (like himself) cannot harm others, but "celui qui les hait veut leur nuire. . . . Les méchans ne sont point dans les deserts, ils sont dans le monde" (D, p. 132).

other solitaries go at your side, unseen, forming a sacred battalion (DQ, p. 18). If we must imitate (envy) someone, let it be a genius in the literary tradition. And our desire for fame? "¿Que es sino darnos a la tradición para vivir en ella y así no morir del todo?" (DQ, p. 24).

5. An Existential Tradition

A man of letters who tells you he scorns
glory is a lying rogue.
UNAMUNO

With the identification of the Rousseau connection we partially satisfied Unamuno's request that, in searching out his spiritual kin, we look beyond his Nietzsches to his Butlers. The unity of the authors' works was revealed by means of the synchronic method of comparatism. The purpose of this method was not to prove that Rousseau's presence in Unamuno's imagination precludes the presence of other figures often associated with the latter's work, nor is the historical overview begun in chapter 1 meant to replace the progress of Rousseauism, noted by Sánchez Barbudo, that links Unamuno to Rousseau through such "sons of Rousseau" as Sénancour and Chateaubriand. We concluded in chapter 1 that Rousseau combines the characteristics of two Renaissance types—the self-glorification of the man of letters, and the self-ridicule of the wise fool—traits which Unamuno perpetuates in his literary quixotism. We may now complete the historical context of the Unamuno-Rousseau relationship by discussing its existentialist setting to help clarify the significance of their unifying experience—herostratism. Since Unamuno from the outset has been recognized as a major existentialist, and Rousseau has even been called the father of existentialism,[1] the congruency of their works with other existentialist writings is to be expected, and is not in itself the point of the following discussion.

Herostratism represents for Unamuno a symptom of the ontological sickness, a thirst for being that is the real goal of all par-

1. Henri Peyre, *Literature and Sincerity* (New Haven, 1963), p. 103.

67

ticular desires. "From it arises envy," he declares, thus naming the vice that prefers to call itself anxiety, a fear of death that causes us to begrudge others their happiness and their existence. Envy is a shadow phenomenon, however, a mediated passion, which is why it is said to be the passion upon which society is founded. We fail to recognize it in ourselves because it is experienced as mockery: for our authors, to feel envy is to feel that one is being ridiculed. Envy and ridicule thus interact in a paranoia in which the actions of others are seen as personal insults. To escape this anguish we sometimes try to convince ourselves that if we could be the envied ones we might be cured, hence we seek fame. Here is the issue for which Rousseau's legend provides a special reference point: what happens to a Herostratus once he becomes famous? Nothing changes. For Rousseau, whose envy is existential, rooted in the human condition, fame is just one more trick or flattering trap concocted by a conspiracy to eliminate his true identity.

The tragicomic sense of life which Unamuno formulates with regard to his malady reflects his participation in a tradition that extends well beyond the presence of Rousseau, and which includes Kierkegaard and Nietzsche, the two figures with whom Unamuno is thought to have most in common.[2] The genius of the modern age, Kierkegaard maintained, is not tragic but comic,[3] a shift which contributes to the problem of the legend (the image others have of us). "To be misunderstood is the height of tragedy," he states. Christ, misunderstood by the people, the Pharisees, even the disciples, represents for Kierkegaard the supreme tragedy, but a tragedy that has become fused with comedy—in the modern era in which tragic man elicits nothing but laughter, Christ has become grotesque. Anguished over the false idea of his personality held by his contemporaries, Kierkegaard identified Christ's tragicomedy with his own: "People laugh and I weep," he complains.[4]

---

2. In any case Kierkegaard and Nietzsche are said to owe direct debts to Rousseau. See Burgelin, pp. 141, 401; Starobinski, *La Transparence*, pp. 42, 54; Jean-Louis Bellenot, "Les Formes de l'Amour dans *La Nouvelle Héloise*," *Annales* (1953–55), pp. 177, 207; W. D. Williams, *Nietzsche and the French* (Oxford, 1952), pp. 103, 126, 142.

3. Charles Glicksberg, *The Tragic Vision in Twentieth-Century Literature* (Carbondale, Ill., 1963), p. 23.

4. Pierre Mesnard, "Is the Category of the 'Tragic' Absent from the Life and Thought of Kierkegaard?" *A Kierkegaard Critique*, ed. Johnson and Thulstrup

Unamuno also feared exposure as a "farsante," feared the confusion of his identity with his disguise, and so determined to "live seriously the comedy of his life" in a way that recalls Kierkegaard's notion of the tragicomic personality (Sánchez Barbudo, p. 128).[5]

Kierkegaard's dilemma echoes Rousseau's problem with the conspiracy of ridicule as well. "If Christ returned to the world today," Kierkegaard says, reiterating Rousseau's identification of his fate with that of a reincarnated Socrates, "they would possibly not put him to death, but instead they would cover him with ridicule. This is martyrdom in the age of reason; in the ages of feeling and passion they put you to death" (Mesnard, p. 113). To retain some semblance of control in this situation, then, one must seek out the mockers and encourage them. Discovering himself thus to be the source of comedy, tragic man, according to Kierkegaard (and Unamuno), must bathe himself in irony to counteract the falsification of his identity (Mounier, pp. 35–36).

Between Rousseau and Unamuno, of course, there intervenes a century of Romantic theory which went so far as to claim that irony was the principle of all art.[6] Humor had become "an inverted and sympathetically laughable form of the sublime, treading 'in the low buskin of comedy' but carrying the tragic mask in her hand, a measure of the finite against the infinite" (Wimsatt, p. 379). Anticipating Nietzsche's "gay science," German writers such as Frederick Schlegel, Jean Paul, and Johann Fichte secularized the transcendental view of theology that measured the vanity of this world against the infinite, and deliberately contrasted the ideal and the real in a self-parody so that even in his awareness of his own folly man could still express his appetite for the boundless. This ironic lucidity, however, is a negative mode of consciousness which can be self-destructive: "Life at its most incandescent phase destroyed itself as it created," Wimsatt says, referring to these ironists in a way that reminds us of the herostratic fire.

(New York, 1962), pp. 109–10. Cf. F. Meyer, "Kierkegaard and Unamuno," RLC 29 (1955); Jesus-Antonio Collado, Kierkegaard y Unamuno (Madrid, 1962).

5. For a convenient summation of the stages in Unamuno's crisis see Blanco-Aguinaga, " 'Authenticity' and the Image," in Unamuno: Creator and Creation, ed. Barcia and Zeitlin (Berkeley, 1967).

6. W. K. Wimsatt, Jr., and Cleanth Brooks, Literary Criticism; A Short History (New York, 1957), pp. 378–80.

With the vision of Zarathustra striding down from his mountain into the market place to harangue an unreceptive public, Nietzsche also establishes a tragicomic spectacle that appeals to Unamuno. Although Paul Ilie states that Unamuno "found nothing serious within himself except his irony," in contrast with Nietzsche's seriousness,[7] Walter Kaufmann considers the general view of a stolid Nietzsche to be a misunderstanding, more legend than fact. In several sections of *The Gay Science* that Kaufmann thinks crucial for an understanding of Nietzsche's world view, we find a discussion of the "comedy of existence" that parallels Unamuno's view. Nietzsche believes that his is still an age of moralities and religions, that is, an age of tragedy. In the long run, however, these serious men and the "short tragedy" will be overwhelmed by laughter from those who recognize the purposelessness of life and we will return to the "eternal comedy."[8] Unamuno furthers this transition from one age to the other. Precisely because we are so grave and serious at bottom, Nietzsche says (like the men of reflexive ridicule), "nothing does us as much good as a *fool's cap*"; we need the dancing, mocking, childish art that is the gay science lest we lose our "freedom above things." To attain this freedom, fool and hero, folly and wisdom must be fused (Nietzsche, p. 164). Although it has been argued that the "specifically Nietzschean character of Unamuno's mind" consists of his use of antithetical or inverse reasoning (Ilie, p. 132), the fact is that Unamuno's effort "to see how things look upside down" is a feature of the wise fool context, a conjunction that points to the modern secularization of certain kinds of religious alienation.

Unamuno, in short, accepts Nietzsche's gay science, the comic cure for the tragic life, but he does not concur with Nietzsche's condemnation of Rousseau as a part of the position. Rousseau, characterized by Nietzsche as "sick with uncontrollable vanity and scorn of himself, this abortion planting himself on the threshold of modern times,"[9] is held responsible for the French Revolution which, Nietzsche felt, gave new impetus to that existential envy—*ressentiment*—initiated by Christian morality and essential to bourgeois values through which the weak triumph over the

7. Paul Ilie, *Unamuno: An Existential View of Self and Society* (Madison, Wis., 1967), p. 275.

8. *The Gay Science*, trans. W. Kaufmann (New York, 1974), p. 75.

9. Williams, p. 128; cf. Nietzsche, *The Will to Power*, trans. Kaufmann and Hollingdale (New York, 1967), p. 63.

strong, corrupting man to the point of self-annihilation. "The fire of a gigantic *ressentiment*," which, following Nietzsche, Max Scheler attributed to Rousseau, is indeed the herostratic fire analyzed by Unamuno. Rather than attacking Rousseau, Unamuno begins to work his way through this modern malady by empathizing with him. In fact, it is precisely Rousseau's association with the French Revolution which Nietzsche so despised that intrigued Unamuno, for not only is that event said to be the greatest manifestation of envy in history, but also, according to Schlegel, the most colossal tragicomedy, the most awe-inspiring grotesquery of the age, combining the terrible and the ridiculous.[10] In Rousseau's writings Unamuno finds the envy, ridiculousness, and "terribility" which he means to summarize in the term "erostratismo." Moreover, with such insights in mind, Unamuno deliberately exploits the Spanish genius for the grotesque and the tragicomic in his search for a genre to embody his vision of a society strangling on resentment. In this sense his work is typical of the era that produced the theatre of the absurd.

The ridiculous, the comedy of self-mockery, has a special function in Unamuno's strategy to cure himself first of all of the herostratic vice. This function may be best understood through a comparison with Sartre's study of Jean Genet. A central point in the study is that man's blunders, errors, failures, his ridiculousness in short, is the experience through which he realizes and actually lives his finitude, his impending death. Voiding all our affairs and efforts, death makes us ridiculous, a reality we must prepare for, Unamuno believes, by making ourselves ridiculous. Seen from Sartre's point of view, then, it is not surprising to find that Rousseau's search for his essence in the *Confessions* consists largely of anecdotes in which he feels foolish, ridiculous, ashamed, since for Sartre such experiences are the very origin of self-consciousness through which we experience our concrete existence, through which we learn of our finitude.[11]

With his heroic embracement of ridicule Unamuno shows that there is no other way to assume and possess the solitude and death revealed in our foolishness, and so to be what we are, than to claim and acclaim our faults, vanities, and blunders. Thus we

10. Wolfgang Kayser, *The Grotesque in Art and Literature*, trans. U. Weisstein (Bloomington, Ind., 1963), p. 51.
11. Sartre, *Being and Nothingness*, trans. H. Barnes (New York, 1956), p. 268.

arouse horror in the hypocritical or self-deluded community and become monsters. But the monster takes his revenge on the community by writing, thus turning his failures and weaknesses into a verbal victory: his words invade the others' subjectivities making them confront the monstrosity (impending death) within themselves. The admission or confession by which this victory is achieved is monstrously difficult to carry out, however, so the writer vacillates between his autistic solitude and the being of a stone, between a preference for his consciousness over the world, and the world over his consciousness, between pride and shame, until finally he is simultaneously the laughing crowd and the terrified victim.[12] If the author can express this dialectic at the heart of human personality, bringing to light "that monstrous and wretched bug which we are likely to become at any moment," he earns his fame by saving us from our vanity, and from our fear of death.

Sartre's example is especially important to the context we are examining since he is the only one besides Unamuno to associate metaphysical desire with Herostratus. In a short story entitled "Erostrate," Sartre applies his interpretation of the Herostratus legend to man's humiliating condition. Horrified by the absurdity of man's vulnerability (the certainty of death), Paul Hilbert contracts a violent rage against his fellow men who seem to be complacently happy. He is encouraged by the example of Herostratus to astonish and confound the world's humanists with an act that would reveal "who I am," that is, what man is really like. His decision to fire a revolver at random into a crowd (destruction without personal benefit) is the modern archetype of absurdity and of a crime of envy as well. At the heart of the story is the same confrontation with mortality, the same ambivalence—the paranoiac fear of the other, the sense of being mocked combined with the need for recognition—that informs this theme in Rousseau and Unamuno. Hilbert's failure to execute his plan successfully is typical of Sartre's view of human behavior, more comic than tragic, in which, in his desire to attain being-in-itself-for-itself (to become God), man resembles an ass in pursuit of a carrot tied just out of reach (Mounier, p. 68).

There is no disagreement among modern existentialists, Camus

12. Sartre, *Saint Genet, Actor and Martyr*, trans. B. Frechtman (New York, 1963), pp. 544–99.

says in this same vein, regarding the definition of man's fundamental problem, which is his "absurdity." The problem is the disproportion between man's intention and the reality he encounters, the contradiction between man's true strength and his aims and desires,[13] the incongruity that informs Romantic irony. Baudelaire thus explains laughter as a demonic recognition of the clash between two dimensions—between man's infinite greatness and his infinite wretchedness. This same contradiction underlies Unamuno's tragicomic sense of life.

Herostratus is for Unamuno what Sisyphus is for Camus—an existential myth. Thus Camus's notion of the absurd defined in *The Myth of Sisyphus* may provide us with a measure of Unamuno's tragicomic sense. Since Camus, like Dostoevski among others, took Don Quixote as a symbol of man's absurd plight,[14] Unamuno's quixotism cannot be said to embody an exclusively Spanish version of the existential crisis. Nonetheless, Unamuno and Camus disagree on two points which differentiate the herostratic from the sisyphean response to absurdity. Camus's absurd man, recognizing his limits, living without appeal, *is indifferent to posterity* (Camus, p. 66). And, quoting with approval a "modern writer" who said "it is essential to be absurd, it is not essential to be a dupe," Camus advises that in the new moral climate we *should not make ourselves ridiculous* (Camus, p. 68). Although as in Unamuno the tragic aspect of man's condition is embodied in a larger comedy, Camus's absurd man is not a clown or fool but a dandy who scorns his fate. Unamuno, on the other hand, takes as his model for modern heroism the humiliated figure of Don Quixote who yearns for fame and who is often the dupe.

The trend we have been discussing in terms of existentialist philosophy has been treated in terms of novelistic literature by

13. Albert Camus, *"The Myth of Sisyphus" and Other Essays*, trans. J. O'Brien (New York, 1967), p. 66.

14. Richard Pearce, in *Stages of the Clown* (Carbondale, Ill., 1970), p. 107, complains that existentialists, although they have the idea of absurdity, fail to realize its comic dimensions. In Unamuno's case, however, it is the critics who have missed the intentionally comic (and grotesque) element in his characterization of the absurd man. Geoffrey Ribbans mistakes Unamuno's creation of grotesque puppets for an inability to create "round" characters, in "The Development of Unamuno's Novels: *Amor y Pedagogía y Niebla*," in *Hispanic Studies in Honor of I. González Llubera* (Oxford, 1959), pp. 269-85. Agnes Moncy finds "no comic characters" in Unamuno and Francisco Ayala sees Alejandro Gomez as comic "in spite of the author." *La Torre* 9 (1961): 355.

René Girard, whose *Deceit, Desire, and the Novel* (Baltimore, 1965), is a "topology" of imitative and metaphysical desire, the historical development of which Girard traces from Cervantes to Dostoevski. Indeed, the resemblance of Girard's insight into the structure of the novel (consisting of triangular desire) to Unamuno's insight into the Herostratus factor in the modern sensibility may be accounted for in part by their mutual use of *Don Quijote* as a point of departure. Girard's excellent study needs to be amended on one point, however, concerning his implication that Unamuno is among the Romantic critics who misunderstood Cervantes's protagonist as a model of autonomy or originality, that is, of spontaneous desire. God being dead, the Romanticist therefore needed to be himself like a god and fostered the illusion of spontaneous desire to conceal from himself the imitative nature of his being (Girard, pp. 16, 98). Unamuno does not harbor such illusions, nor do his writings "passively reflect" mediation, but actively reveal it, indicating that he is in Girard's terms a "novelesque" writer—one who transcends the ontological sickness through his writing. With his tactic of reflexive ridicule and his rejection of Rousseau's attempt at an autonomous solitude, Unamuno shows that he has overcome the terrible fear of ridicule which Girard (following Stendhal) identifies as the principal feature of "la vanité triste" predominant in the nineteenth century. Described as "self-surgery, without any anesthetic but the work itself" (ST, p. 278), Unamuno's confessions transcend "the two pedantries"—the sentimental (Romantic) and the rationalistic—in a final vision that encompasses both Don Quixote's madness and Alonso Quixano's repentance. The great novelistic writers, Girard says, using Proust's concluding recovery of lost time as a paradigm (foreshadowed by Quixote's deathbed conversion), reconcile romantic illusion and novelistic disenchantment in a final escape from the vicious circle of self-centeredness and other-directedness. Unamuno's experience verifies Girard's position. In the light of Girard's theory about the function of envy in narrative structure, we can see why so many of Unamuno's fictions are a reliving of Don Quixote's death, since there is nothing Unamuno wants more than to defeat envy in modern society, in Spain, and especially in himself. The protagonist's death represents the author's cure.

And yet it is not quite as simple as that, for however much Una-

muno and Rousseau protest the evils, or at least the "wretchedness" of Herostratus, they both pursue literary fame, the practice
of letters being as often a manifestation of the herostratic passion
as it is a cure of this passion. The Rousseau with whom Unamuno
empathizes is the one who announces that "the role I have chosen
of writing and remaining in the background is precisely the one
that suits me. If I had been present, people would not have known
my value." It is the Rousseau who declared, "Let the last trump
sound when it will, I shall come forward with this work in my
hand, to present myself before my Sovereign Judge, and proclaim
aloud: 'Here is what I have done' " (Cohen, p. 17). How much herostratism is there in this intention? Compare the resemblance of the
authors' opposition to progress in the arts and sciences with Herostratus's destruction of one of the seven wonders of the world.
Each one's project is to destroy some part of man's cultural
treasure—Rousseau attacks writing by writing, Unamuno, with his
game theory, attacks logic with logic (they write against writing,
or reason against reasoning). Each attacks a mode of human
achievement from within, in short, as Herostratus must have gone
inside the temple to find the areas most vulnerable to flame. Consumed thus by a self-contradiction, *which is the common source of
the tragic and the grotesque*, the authors extend our understanding
of Herostratus's legendary act: not the self, but only the legend
survives the "deed," just as Herostratus must have perished in the
burning temple.

In the same way that Herostratus was consumed in his fire, the
author's life (or self) is sacrificed to his book. Literature is death,
Unamuno points out, but a death in which others may find life:
"Because whoever reads a novel may live it and relive it . . ."
(CSH, p. 88). Don Quixote must die in disillusionment, he says,
so that Sancho may live on "in life-giving illusion" (DQ, p. 219).
Translated into the author's situation, this idea becomes Unamuno's declaration, "Death to me! Long live my fame!" for in
the author's fame the reader finds the inspiration to live. Unamuno's logic here is based on his own experience, involving his
response to the question of whether it is possible to live noncom-
paratively. Georg Simmel, following Nietzsche, believed that
the "noble man" refuses to compare himself and instead enjoys
a naïve self-confidence in his own worth prior to any mediated
desires. Hence he is untroubled by the merits of others. Max

Scheler denies that such a stance is possible, noting that all values are comparative, that therefore only a "unique buffoon" could live free of comparison.[15] Scheler's solution to the resentment that arises from comparative living is the same as Rousseau's—to imitate God rather than other men (which turns out to be itself a buffoon-like stance). Unamuno, realizing that he cannot avoid mediation, and being unable in the twentieth century to follow Rousseau's example, chooses a mediator with enough distance from himself to at least reduce the pain of envy (the closer the other whose desires we imitate the greater the anxiety, in Girard's terms). In fact, like Don Quixote's choice of Amadis, Unamuno's choice is an example of external mediation—a model that is outside his own "world." He imitates, that is, the great authors in the literary tradition. "Our desperate struggle to perpetuate our name extends backward into the past, just as it pushes forward into the conquest of the future. We battle with the dead, who put the living into the shade. We are envious of past genius, of those whose names, like landmarks in History, loom across the centuries" (ST, p. 52).[16] Far from wanting to conceal this mediation (the corrupting lie), he declares it openly and is raised up by it, finding in it an inspiration and a consolation. Thus he imitates the happiness of being an Author the way Rousseau imitated the happiness of God.

To sacrifice one's self to one's fame is the quintessence of quixotism which finally makes it indistinguishable (or nearly so) from herostratism, for this sacrifice is exactly what Rousseau hated about the illness of his age—the sacrifice of the present, living self to an image or opinion in the public mind. He condemned the vocation of letters because he thought of the pursuit of fame as the desire for public approval.[17] In fact, he considered his own

15. Scheler, "*Ressentiment*," trans. W. Holdheim (New York, 1961), pp. 52–54.

16. *The Selected Works of Miguel de Unamuno*, vol. 4, trans. A. Kerrigan (Princeton, 1972), p. 60.

17. See Lionel Trilling, *Sincerity and Authenticity* (Cambridge, Mass., 1971), p. 60. In this regard it is significant that Sartre's account of Genet's initial encounter with the master-slave struggle involved in public opinion and the identity crisis parallels Rousseau's experience. Both Rousseau and Genet are set off on the personality quest that leads them eventually to become writers by childhood incidents when they were "surprised by shame." Labeled "thief," each became a thief. Here we have the problem of the legend: caught in the abyss that separates their subjective certainty of self from their objective truth for others, both men feel innocent yet judge themselves guilty.

career justified because he did not court public approval, but violated the received ideas of his time at every opportunity. Unfortunately, it is this very notoriety which makes his efforts herostratic.

Unamuno's attempted evasion of the accusation of herostratism has a different rationale: he could not be accused of sacrificing his living, essential self to a shadow image since he asserts that there is no essential self until it is invented in writing. Thus he always takes the side of Don Quixote against Cervantes. The fictional character is more real than the historical author because the real is what "works," what acts in the world—it is Don Quixote who lives in our imagination, not Cervantes. It would be better, he asserts, if *Don Quijote* was anonymous, without any recollection of Cervantes (in whom the author was vastly superior to the man) to interfere with our relationship to the character. But we may perceive in his cruelty to the memory of Cervantes a kind of masochism (and not only because he carefully avoids Cervantes's "mistake" of creating a mythical character, choosing an autobiographical method instead), for elsewhere he admits that Don Quixote's desire for fame is Cervantes's desire. Dulcinea represents Glory for Unamuno as well as Cervantes. He is less concerned with influencing his contemporaries than with having his name *live after him*.[18] If a choice were forced on any author, Unamuno adds, between whether his name or his works should perish, the work would always be sacrificed.

The position he takes on this issue depends on whether he is thinking as a reader or a writer. But more and more Unamuno tends to think as a reader, to think about the readers who might relive his works in the future. Would he then appreciate the irony, do you suppose, in the position taken by contemporary literary theorists with regard to his phenomenological gamble? The ontological illness generated by the death of God for man—the definitive context for all Unamuno's thought—causes Unamuno not to abandon the theological model of the creative act, but to invert it. God's creation of man is not the model, but the reflection of man's creation of art; divine immortality is not the model but the shadow of worldly fame. Thus Unamuno totally commits

---

18. Rousseau makes it clear in the first *Discourse* that he is writing for the Ages, and despises men who write for popularity. Unamuno's position is the same. *The Selected Works of Miguel de Unamuno*, vol. 3, trans. A. Kerrigan (Princeton, 1967), pp. 361, 358.

himself to the life of his works in a literary tradition. He wagers that the consciousness generated by reading is as much the author's as the reader's, so that in the apparent immortality of fame it may be possible, physiologically possible even, to experience a personal perpetuation in the consciousness of others. How would he react, then, to the current theoreticians of literature, such as the members of the *Tel Quel* school, who, in following the logic of the death of God to its ultimate conclusion, have announced the death of the author as well?[19] It is not enough, they assert, to stop with the inversion of the theological model of meaning; it must be abandoned altogether.

A representative example of such theories is Roland Barthes's "The Death of the Author" (*Aspen*, 1967), in which he points out that "linguistics has just furnished the destruction of the Author with a precious analytic instrument by showing that utterance in its entirety is a void process, which functions perfectly without requiring to be filled by the person of the interlocutors." Consequently representation disappears, replaced by a simple "performative" in which utterance has no other content than the act by which it is uttered: "the modern writer is born simultaneously with his text." There is no single "theological" meaning (the "God-Author's" message); a text is never "closed," so that writing "liberates an activity which we might call counter-theological, properly revolutionary, for to refuse to arrest meaning is finally to refuse God and his hypostases, reason, science, law."

We read on one of Unamuno's pages the words "I do not want to die!" These words have no origin, in Barthes's view, that is, their true locus is the reader. The reader writes the text, unifies it by being the field in which all the threads, voices, citations of the writing may be gathered together. "The birth of the reader must be ransomed by the death of the author." Enough has been said already to indicate that Unamuno would not be disturbed by any of the statements quoted so far, for he was working towards a similar position in a "text" like *Como se hace una novela*. Participating in that very refusal of God and his hypostases mentioned by Barthes, Unamuno declares writing to be a process, not a product, in which the reader takes the author's part, in which the meaning remains open, in which the words are a surface without depth, or

19. Jean-Louis Baudry, "Ecriture, Fiction, Idéologie," in *Théorie d'Ensemble* (Paris, 1968), p. 137.

rather, a surface in which the illusion of depth is a transparent mask (CSH, pp. 185, 194, 196). "Language is what gives us reality, and it does so not as a mere vehicle of reality, but as the true flesh of reality" (ST, p. 270). With textual theory, Barthes notes, "the enunciation's sincerity, which has been a veritable 'cross' of literary morality, becomes a false problem,"[20] which is why Unamuno adopted a concept similar to what we now call "writing" instead of "literature," one in which the distance between writing and reading is radically reduced, in which, as Barthes says, life is a fable that runs concurrent with the work (or as Unamuno states it, "vivo ahora y aquí mi vida contándola").

Although exact parallels could be established between Barthes's theory of the text and Unamuno's aesthetics, this is not the place to discuss the continuity between existentialist and structuralist literature. Rather, we have extended the context of our theme to include contemporary theory in order to bring out the implications of Unamuno's position, that is, a world view from which the agony of Herostratus would be absent. When he says that all his writings are political he implies something like what Phillipe Sollers has described as the revolutionary element in "writing," a theory that in its attack on bourgeois literature—its deconstruction of the myths of "author" and "work"—represents a devaluation of the bourgeois ideology in general. What this means for Unamuno and the authors in the tradition in which he is working is the end of envy, the motivating vice of bourgeois culture. Barthes reminds us that the concept of the "author" arose at the time of the Renaissance as a corollary of the individualism that accompanied the growing power of the middle class. And with it arose that extreme form of envy—*ressentiment*—which Unamuno considers to be the tragedy of Spain (CSH, p. 107). It is in this specific context of values that Unamuno confesses his envy and vanity, in order to liberate his "medieval soul" from the Renaissance, Reformation, and Revolution that have shaped modern man: "Quixotism is simply the most desperate phase of the battle of the Middle Ages against its offspring the Renaissance" (ST, p. 279). And yet he is a modern man whose professed aim "is to make all men live a life of restless longing." To the extent that he succeeds, his books are an act of revenge of which Herostratus would approve.

20. Barthes, "De l'oeuvre au texte," *Revue d'esthétique* 3 (1971).

UNIVERSITY OF FLORIDA MONOGRAPHS

Humanities